G. Part of y̆ Suburbs of y̆ City of Naples
H. A Fiery Current running into y̆ Sea
I. Smoak proceeding from y̆ Fiery Current
K. Monte Nivosi towards Apulia
L. Vineyards Gardens of Oranges, Lemon͂s.

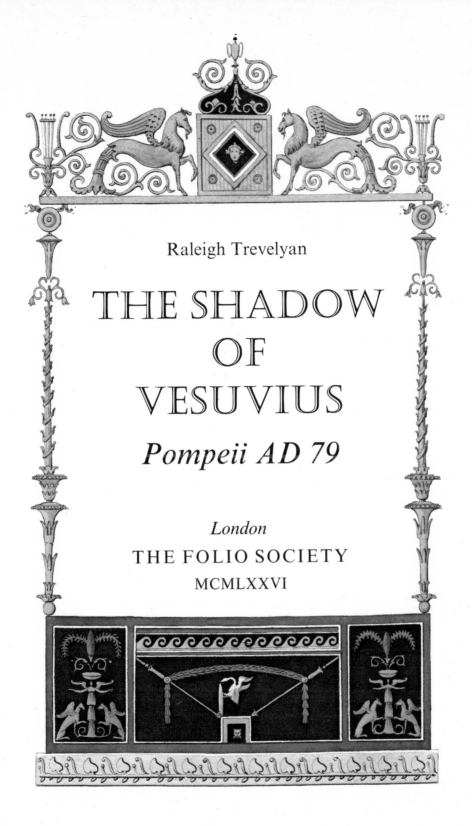

Raleigh Trevelyan

THE SHADOW OF VESUVIUS

Pompeii AD 79

London
THE FOLIO SOCIETY
MCMLXXVI

PRINTED IN GREAT BRITAIN
Printed and bound by Jarrold & Sons Ltd, Norwich
Set in 11 point 'Monophoto' Times New Roman, spaced 2 points

CONTENTS

ACKNOWLEDGEMENTS

I must first of all thank John Letts for asking me to write this book, and for his constant encouragement and enthusiasm; and Sara Ellis for her inspired picture research. Raul Balin has also been of great assistance to me. I owe a considerable debt to Dr Alda Croce, Signora Silvia Cammarano Croce and Signora Lidia Herling Croce for introductions in Naples, and to Professoressa Maria Annechino for arranging a memorable visit round Stabiae and Oplontis. Dr George Walker of the Imperial Institute has been very patient with my questions on matters of geology and has guided me to useful sources. I am also grateful for information and help from Sheila Bishop, Edith Clay, Barone Corsi, J. M. Edmonds, John Fleming, Brian Fothergill, Reynold Higgins, Hugh Honour, Peter Jolly, Eric de Maré, Ia C. McIlwaine, John Ward-Perkins, Commendatore G. Ruggiero, Dr Luigi Santoro, Alexander Walker and Ann Whitaker. The extracts from Pliny's letters are adapted from the Bosanquet translation; the Dio Cassius quotations are from the Foster version. When quoting from Goethe's *Italian Journey* I have in some instances used phrases from the Auden-Meyer translation (Collins, London, 1962).

The following is a short list of some of the works which I have found particularly useful, in addition to standard sources.

J. H. d'Arms, *Romans in the Bay of Naples*, London, 1970.
Arts Council, *The Age of Neo-classicism*, catalogue of Royal Academy Exhibition, London, 1972.
Marcel Brion, *Pompeii and Herculaneum*, London, 1960.
Fred M. Bullard, *Volcanoes in History, in Theory, in Eruption*, Edinburgh, 1962.
Jérôme Carcopino, *Daily Life in Ancient Rome*, London, 1941.
S. N. Coleman, *Volcanoes New and Old*, London, 1949.
Edward Croft-Murray, *Decorative Painting in England*, London, 1970.
Matteo Della Corte, *Case ed abitanti di Pompei*, Rome, 1954.
Egon C. C. Corti, *The Death and Resurrection of Herculaneum and Pompeii*, London, 1951.
Alfonso De Franciscis, *La pittura pompeiana*, Florence, 1968.
Alfonso De Franciscis, *The Pompeian Wall Paintings in Oplontis*, Recklinghausen, 1975.
Joseph Jay Deiss, *Herculaneum*, London, 1968.
John Fleming, *Robert Adam and his Circle*, London, 1962.
Brian Fothergill, *Sir William Hamilton*, London, 1969.
Mabel M. Gabriel, *Masterpieces of Campanian Painting*, New York, 1952.
Geological Society of America Bulletin, V. 84, pp. 759–772, March 1973, *Two Plinian Pumice-Fall Deposits from Somma-Vesuvius, Italy*.
Michael Grant, *Cities of Vesuvius from Somma-Vesuvius, Italy*.
Michael Grant, *Eros a Pompei*, Milan, 1974.
H.M.S.O., *Works of Art in Italy: Losses and Survival in the War*, London, Part I 1945, Part II 1946.
Hugh Honour, *Neo-classicism*, London, 1968.
Giuseppina Cerulli Irelli, *Ercolano*, Naples, 1969.
Jack Lindsay, *The Writing on the Wall*, London, 1960.
Wolfgang Lippman, *Pompeii in Fact and Fiction*, London, 1968.
J. Logan Lobley, *Mount Vesuvius*, London, 1889 ed.
George A. Macdonald, *Volcanoes*, London, 1972.
Amedeo Maiuri, *Passeggiate campane*, Florence, 1950.
Amedeo Maiuri, *Pompeii*, Novara, 1957. Official guide-book, Rome, 1961.
Amedeo Maiuri, *Ercolano*, official guide-book, Rome, 1970.
August Mau, *Pompeii, its Life and Art*, London and New York, 1899.
Clifford Musgrave, *Adam and Hepplewhite and other Neo-classical Furniture*, London, 1966.
Mario Praz, *An Illustrated History of Interior Decoration*, London, 1964.
Mario Praz, *On Neoclassicism*, London, 1969.
A. Rittman, *Volcanoes and their Activity*, London and New York, 1962.
Villa Hügel, *Pompeji: Leben und Kunst in den Vesuvstädten*, catalogue of exhibition, Essen, 1973.
Waldstein and Shoobridge, *Herculaneum, Past, Present and Future*, London, 1908.
J. B. Ward-Perkins, *Cities of Ancient Greece and Italy*, London, 1974.
Peter Weiner, *Pompeji und die Wanddekoration der Goethezeit*, Munich, 1970.
Sir Mortimer Wheeler, *Roman Art and Architecture*, London, 1964.

INTRODUCTION

Most books on Pompeii are concerned with what it must have been like to have lived there. This one is mainly about the impact of its rediscovery on individuals, an impact which in turn has had effects on art, taste and literature.

It is also a personal book, and as such I have attempted to make it an introduction to the sites for the newcomer, with an emphasis on particular places and objects that created excitement and wonder when they were first unearthed. I have also related the story to the erratic behaviour of the *genius loci,* Mount Vesuvius.

The subject is vast and this is a short book, so I have had to deal summarily with what might be called the middle (and in certain ways less dramatic) period of the excavations. I have relied on the illustrations to show some of the influence of the broadly termed Pompeian style in art and decoration.

Finally this book is not just to do with Pompeii, but with all the places that were overwhelmed in the catastrophe of AD 79. To visit them arouses many contrasting emotions, and this is their perennial fascination. They also make one feel – uncomfortably perhaps – that a span of nineteen centuries is not so very long after all.

2. *Visitors at the Temple of Isis, 1778–9.*

3. *The last eruption of Vesuvius, March 1944.*

I

THE MURDEROUS MOUNTAIN

The last time Vesuvius erupted was in March 1944. A cycle had ended, and after a while the yellow genista began to spring up again among the rocks of old lava flows. Previously, for just over three centuries, this most famous of all volcanoes had never remained quiet for more than seven years. The ordinary visitor nowadays is therefore entitled to regard such an extended period of dormancy as sinister, even though the watchers at the Observatory are reassuringly calm – and this in spite of recent tremors and earth movements at Pozzuoli and the Phlegraen Fields, which are obviously in some way connected with Vesuvius.

The cycle actually began in 1631 with an explosion almost as violent as the one which overwhelmed Pompeii and Herculaneum in AD 79. Another 'paroxysmal' eruption occurred in 1767; thereafter others followed at frequent intervals – in 1779, 1794, 1822, 1838, 1850, 1872, 1906 and finally 1944. In between were several other minor outbreaks, sometimes in successive years. After a period of rest, cone-building would begin and the funnel of the volcano would become blocked. Pressure would then build up, resulting in earthquakes and lava flows. Then would come the great blow-off and the umbrella pine-shaped cloud which we now commonly associate with the dropping of atom bombs.

Until AD 79 people had not realized that Vesuvius was a volcano, although some remarks by Strabo about fire-blackened stones seem to show that he had his suspicions. The huge crater had become filled with vines and undergrowth through which wild boars roamed, and it was here that Spartacus and his slave army were able to take refuge. There had been one extremely severe earthquake in AD 62. This had been a warning, but – understandably perhaps – it had not been heeded.

Vesuvius may be quiet, but it is by no means dead. Scorching hot *fumarole*, smelling of sulphur, still seep from the crater, and tremors are frequently recorded, deep in the magma chamber, reckoned to be some five kilometres below sea-level. What devilry is the double-humped old monster plotting?

I first saw Vesuvius a short while before its final eruption. I was then a very young infantry subaltern arriving by troopship from Algiers. Having always loved those early nineteenth-century gouaches of the bay – either night scenes with jagged flashes from the volcano, or seascapes, pink and white, with Vesuvius

4. *The Forum at Pompeii today.*

smoking dutifully away in the background, and in front little fisher-boats idling round the Castel dell'Ovo – I was taken aback to find Naples wretchedly bomb-scarred and under snow, and Vesuvius itself looking as though it were made of dirty china clay. There was that skein of smoke all right, floating eastwards from the cone. Like a flag on a castle that announces the chieftain's presence, so a traveller wrote exactly a hundred years before. But it was not as big as I expected, and I was surprised to notice so many houses scattered on the mountain's slopes.

Within a week, the sun having returned, some friends and I caught the delightfully named little train, the Circumvesuviana, to Pompeii. We were determined to enjoy ourselves and took with us a copy of Charles Dickens' *Pictures from Italy* and some bottles of Lacrima Cristi wine.

Herculaneum was barred to us, as was the Naples Museum (which ideally should be visited first) – since, we were told, the best of its contents were safely stored in the Vatican. Indeed the only way of getting into some sites at Pompeii, after breaking through the phalanx of sellers of cameos, coral necklaces, fountain pens, winged phalluses and dirty postcards, was to bribe custodians with cigarettes. We had no wish that day, with the front line only a few score miles away, to be reminded that all things on earth are transitory, the first and obvious impression that strikes any visitor to Pompeii. It was hard too to ignore the fact that the Allies had dropped at least 150 bombs on the ruins, in the belief that the Germans were using them as an ammunition dump. We wanted to visualize the place as a city of life, teeming, noisy and rather vulgar, commercially thriving, but designed also for pleasure and entertainment. Strangely enough, we found that when Dickens went to Pompeii in 1845 Vesuvius then had also been 'bright and snowy in the peaceful distance'. In his book he instructed us to stand in the Forum and admire it through the columns of the Temples of Isis and Jupiter, and this we dutifully did, forcing ourselves to see it simply as a thing of beauty, not of 'doom and destiny, biding its terrible time'. And beautiful it was indeed with the clouds' violet shadows moving across the melting snow.

We drank our wine on the steps of the amphitheatre. Here Bulwer Lytton had made the evil Egyptian Arbaces face the lion at the very moment the eruption began. How difficult it was to shut our minds to the horrors of 79! In the year 59, our guide told us, there had been a riot in this amphitheatre between rival Pompeian and Nucerian gladiator fans, as a result of which the Roman Senate had banned contests for ten years. We approved of that decision. Twenty thousand people could have sat here. Perhaps the equivalent of Pompeii's entire population. And now this silence. The streets outside were made of great

5. *The Forum at Pompeii 120 years ago.*

octagonal blocks of lava. As we walked down the Street of Abundance, we were very taken by the deep chariot ruts. Did nobody care about road repairs in those days? Surely, being so narrow, these streets must have been one way? If not, and if Pompeians were anything like modern Neapolitans, imagine the yells and arguments between drivers. The stepping-stones across seemed to show that the streets must have been filthy too, and no doubt smelly, which come to think of it was odd, the Romans being so keen on personal cleanliness.

Pompeians were prize defacers of walls. Lovers' scrawls, shop advertisements, election propaganda, in strange long letters very close together. 'The Muleteers support C. Julius Polybius for Praetor.' 'Victoria, wherever you are, may your sneeze bring you luck.' A gladiator was the *suspirum puellarum*, the girls' heart-throb. And in a doss-house: 'My host, I've wet my bed. I confess my sin. Why, you ask? Because there was no pot.' Phalluses for sign-posts. Or were they there, as the guide assured us, simply against the evil eye? Little shop slabs in rooms built into large *palazzi*. Just like Naples, or Algiers. The ordinary people certainly lived in absurdly small houses.

Bakers' ovens. Amphoras on racks. A dog barking in mosaic. The sign of a goat above a dairy. Still this unsettling silence. It was like a game of Shadows.

6. *The Small Theatre, or Odeon, at Pompeii.*

7. *Cart ruts and stepping-stones at Pompeii.*

You jump round, but the person behind has been too smart for you. He stands there, one foot lifted, face rigid, immobile. Only in this case he is also invisible. Immobile for eternity. Unless the bombers come back to set him free.

'Ramble on,' Dickens advised us, 'and see at every turn the little familiar tokens of human habitation and everyday pursuits; the chafing of the bucket-rope in the stone rim of the exhausted well ... the marks of drinking-vessels on the stone counters of wine-shops.' Fish-sauce, tufa, fruit, wine, millstones; these were the main exports of Pompeii. The sea was much closer in those days. A pleasure of living in the town, compared to the alleys of modern Naples, must have been the great, glorious views on all sides; the Bay and Capri, the mountains of the Sorrento peninsula, and of course old Vesuvius.

We rambled, reaching the Odeon, a covered theatre for concerts that had only held a thousand people. It must have been one of the few public places in Pompeii that had been quiet. Beyond was the Large Theatre, equipped for five thousand spectators. 'This house won't pay,' Mark Twain had remarked. Three bombs had been dropped on it. Beyond that again were the gladiators' barracks, where sixty-three skeletons had been found, some shackled together by the ankle. The guide showed us pictures of armour and helmets, as rich and fantastic as drawings by Leonardo da Vinci. Also in the barracks, he told us with a nudge, a jewelled skeleton of a woman had been found: caught in the act.

The word Pompeii had nothing to do with Pompey, as we so ignorantly had supposed. It had an Oscan origin. The Oscans were an ancient Italic people

Luigi Bazzani
POMPEI . 1895

8. *The House of the Vettii,
1895.*

who had been in this area before the Greek traders. They had been followed
by Etruscans, then Samnites. Both Pompeii and Herculaneum (originally
Heracleion, after Heracles) had rebelled against Rome. The marks of Sulla's
siege can still be seen on the walls of Pompeii . . . It is three quarters of a mile from
one end of the town to the other . . . Before long the most ardent and Lacrima
Cristi-fortified sightseer begins to flag, and we found it a relief to enter the
arcaded gardens of large houses, such as that of the *nouveaux riches* brothers
Vettii (excavated fifty years after Dickens' visit). Those lines of fractured,
roofless, windowless boxes outside were beginning to seem as if they were
stretching to Sorrento. First of all, naturally, at the entrance of the Vettii house,
the guide unveiled for us the famous fresco of the calf-length phallus, 'worth its
weight in gold', and looking – this time to quote Malcolm Lowry – like Cyrano de

Bergerac's nose. Not for the *signorina* in our party. But what about Pompeian *signorine*? There had been no such concern for their prudery, to judge by what we had seen from the postcards. A big phallus was everybody's joke in AD 79.

The *atrium* of the house led into the beautiful garden or peristyle, with translucent alabaster basins; in between each of the columns there had been a bronze or marble statue in the form of a fountain. From the size of root-holes it had been deduced what plants had grown here, and these very plants had been replaced in the garden. More bomb damage, alas. In the *triclinium* or dining-room we looked at the busy winged cupids painted on a broad black background, contrasting so dramatically with the celebrated red which is now so difficult to match. Cupids squashing grapes, driving chariots drawn by goats and dolphins, bartering oil and wine. *Trompe l'œil* peacocks sitting above. The whole house was like an art gallery. Bacchus and Ariadne. Apollo and Daphne. Amazons. Satyrs. Jupiter enthroned. All obviously painted by different hands, and all painted after the earthquake of 62. Then a *lararium,* a shrine for household gods, and a small room with crudely drawn sex-scenes, leading, strangely, off the kitchen.

Next door was the House of the Golden Cupids, with another charming garden, a little shrine to Isis and pillars decorated with sea-monsters. The House of the Tragic Poet was pretty, too, with a peculiar fresco of Venus looking at a

9. *A main street in Pompeii.*

nest of cupids; this was Glaucus' house in the *Last Days*. These big, inward-looking houses of the wealthy made one think of the Casbah in Algiers. They had been designed for peace and coolness.

Dickens mentioned the Villa of Diomede, so we had to seek it out, beyond the town walls and near the Street of the Tombs ('Goethe sat there,' the guide said proudly, pointing at a seat by the tomb of the priestess Mamia). The villa had a huge view of the sea and coast. Its garden was over a hundred feet square and was surrounded by colonnades, and in the centre were a fish-pool and an arbour that had been used as a summer dining-room. The owner had built himself a private bathroom, rare in Pompeii where there existed at least four public bath buildings. In contrast to the Vettii's house all the frescoes had been removed to the Naples Museum.

The Villa of Diomede had been excavated in 1771–4. As Dickens reminded us, eighteen skeletons of women and children had been found in the vault. They had brought food in the hope that it would sustain them until the eruption ended. But the ashes had easily found their way down there, and the shapes of their bodies had been found with clothes wrapped round the faces. A man, possibly the villa's owner, had been discovered near the garden door, with a key in his hand; behind him there had been a slave, holding money and other valuables. Bulwer Lytton had made Diomede beg for help from fleeing passers-by; 'I am Diomed – ten thousand sesterces to him who helps me!' It had been the discovery of a young girl's skeleton, with a well-developed bosom and thigh impressed in the hardened ash, that had inspired Théophile Gautier's ghostly story *Arria Marcella* in 1852.

The greatest and most disturbing sight of all at Pompeii, the Villa of the Mysteries – even larger, with sixty rooms downstairs alone – was also denied to Dickens, having been excavated between 1909 and 1910 and 1929 and 1930; and unfortunately to us too in those days of war. It had to be reserved for a much later visit.

By and large most of the paintings remaining at Pompeii (as distinct from those in the Museum) are less remarkable as works of art than for their curious subject-matter, their colours, vigour, gaiety, use of perspective, occasional impressionistic technique and the clues they provide to styles of architecture, furniture and clothing. An interesting thing about them is that there are so many, even in the houses of people in the lowest social scale. It has been remarked that the only real comparison that can be made is with the Dutch of the sixteenth and seventeenth centuries, and even then the Dutch went in for easel paintings. The ordinary Pompeians lived mostly out of doors or went to public buildings for their entertainment, so their houses were kept small, and the frescoes were therefore intended to give an illusion of space. Thus what one is mostly looking at is popular art in a straightforward, if earthy, commercial town.

Whoever had the Villa of the Mysteries decorated, however, was neither

10. *The House of Cornelius Rufus, 1930.*

straightforward nor poor, and the frescoes in the main room are by an artist who, though not a genius, would stand out in any century. Those darting, fearful eyes, those crowded figures, those hints of obscenity and ritual, those rich dark colours. That sidelong, knowing smile of the satyr in the ante-room. Silenus' hostile stare. The terror of the maiden about to feel the lash on her bared flesh; her sweaty hair. The triumphant cymbals. For all the suggestion of lesbianism we are supposed to be witnessing the initiation ceremony for young brides to Dionysiac mysteries. At the end we see an enthroned woman, presumably the villa's mistress, satisfied with the pain and shock she has perpetrated. It would seem that this woman abandoned the place after the earthquake of 62 (or died about then?) and that the new owner, a Greek freedman called Zosimus, had more bucolic tastes. The resulting contrast in atmosphere adds to the villa's strangeness. There is pathos as well, for here the skeleton of a porter was found, staunchly at his post while all the world was being smothered. Then, in the peristyle, a statue of Augustus' wife Livia has been unearthed, rather severe, with a very Roman nose and dressed like a priestess, a contrast in mood to the whipping ladies in that inner room; she had not yet been erected when the ash came and was discovered propped against a wall. Bodies like the porter's became decomposed within a hardish shell of pumice powder and ash, thus leaving their exact shapes. It had been Giuseppe Fiorelli, one of the great names in the history of the excavations, who in the last century discovered a way of making plaster moulds out of the shells. So now one can see the full nightmare of the ultimate loneliness of death by suffocation, from the writhing of a chained dog to lovers reaching out towards one another and women sprawled face downwards with their skirts rucked up to their waists.

We left, that February day in 1944, as the long shadows of cypresses were beginning to reach out in the Street of the Tombs. Suddenly, in the slightly orange light, Pompeii became very beautiful. Our feelings perhaps were more mixed than Dickens' had been. For one thing, we had been able to see the place as a civic whole, complete with public baths, gymnasium, public meeting places, temples, shops, large merchants' houses. Less was left to our imagination. This was how an ancient people had lived, from day to day. We had been instructed.

Then, as we were soldiers, it had been assumed by the guide that we were only really interested in seeing or hearing about erotica; presumably not the case with Dickens' guide in 1845. We were rather baffled by the Pompeian attitude towards

11. *Shape of a corpse preserved in plaster by Fiorelli.*

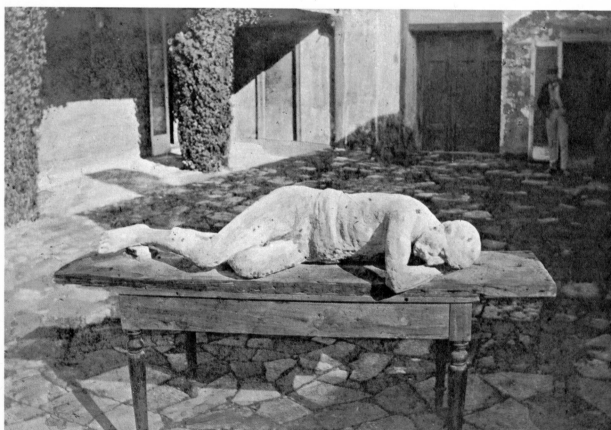

sex. Obviously it was uninhibited and therefore no doubt 'healthy'; but wasn't it also a bit obsessive? All right, Venus and Dionysus were worshipped at Pompeii, and Priapus was the god of gardens. Even so, the attitude appeared to have been pretty light-hearted – dare one say blasphemous? Or was Pompeii the Brighton of the Bay of Naples, where you bought a winged phallus instead of a rude card of a fat lady in a bathing suit?

We were also young, and trying to make ourselves shrug off whatever ordeals might be ahead of us – at Cassino, the Volturno and Anzio. I think we each secretly realized that our visit to Pompeii had not helped in this. We could not but feel overwhelmed by the thought of yet more contorted bodies waiting to be uncovered, and of fantastic new treasures lurking deep under the pumice dust, as important perhaps as the Alexander mosaic, the Boscoreale silver and the Herculaneum bronzes. And we still had so much to see: the House of the Faun, reckoned by Michael Grant to be 'more imposing than any known palace or villa of contemporary Hellenistic kings'; and the Houses of the Silver Wedding and Menander, both post-Dickens' day.

Sometime, too, Herculaneum lay ahead for us. Not that Dickens had seen any more than the perplexing, dark underground passages that eighteenth-century workmen had made, for him simply a 'disordered dream'. Herculaneum had been a much smaller place than Pompeii, less mercantile, more residential. No chariot ruts or stepping-stones there. A great deal of it still lies under the modern town of Resina. For its fate had been quite different to Pompeii's. Whilst Pompeii had been buried in layers of pumice dust, *lapilli* and ash, mixed with fragments of rock, to a depth of twenty-five feet, Herculaneum had been submerged by a vast, sticky mudflow, up to fifty feet deep. The people of Pompeii had been asphyxiated or else crushed by falling rocks or ceilings, but at Herculaneum the inhabitants had mostly had time to escape. Pompeii is easier to excavate, but the mud of Herculaneum has solidified into the consistency of rock. Moreover, this mud is a better preservative than Pompeii's covering. Wooden beams and furniture, papyrus rolls and even carbonized food have been found in some quantity at Herculaneum. When Sir Walter Scott went to Pompeii at the very end of his life, he wandered round the ruins muttering 'City of the Dead, City of the Dead'. He would not have been quite so oppressed if he had been able to see the twentieth-century excavations at Herculaneum.

Early in March I was sent to the Front, so I missed the eruption that began on the 12th and lasted until the 29th.

The first thing I noticed, on my return in June, was that Vesuvius had altered in shape. In February the cone could easily be seen from Naples. Now the top was flat. Indeed the whole mountain seemed lower, and lopsided. What I thought were puffs of smoke were, I was told, simply dust-clouds. Vesuvius had to all

12. *Night view of Vesuvius erupting, March 1944.*

intents gone to sleep. All the same there was some nervousness about earthquakes.

The danger, as always from the point of view of ash, had been on the windward side, the south-east, as in 79. At the Observatory they had noticed as early as 1 March that the usual tremors were dwindling. Then on the 12th the cone collapsed. Flames were visible from below. 'In my ignorance,' a friend had written to me, 'we thought these very romantic and quite normal.' She was working as a Sister at the 103rd General Hospital at Nocera, on the site of the ancient Nuceria and thirteen miles from Vesuvius. For some days nobody seemed to think that anything much would happen, in spite of the fact that in Naples by night you could see a large incandescent lava flow snaking down the side, and that it had swept away the funicular railway.

'When we woke on the morning of the eruption [i.e. the blow-off on the 21st],' my friend continued, 'it was extremely dark like a foggy winter morning, and at first we thought it was going to snow. When we got downstairs there was a group of village women, who used to come every day to take our laundry, and they were all wailing "*Vesuvio! Vesuvio!*"'

Black ash, like a hail of burnt rice grains, fell on Nocera for several hours. They were quite cool however. Anxiously the hospital staff waited for the pungent (and fatal) gases which can accompany a paroxysmal eruption. Meanwhile there were more lava flows down the mountain, and the largest – white-hot, orange-gold, spotted with black, undulating like waves and moving at the rate of a hundred yards an hour – cut through the little towns of Massa and San Sebastiano on the north slope.

Naples was spared the darkness by day, and at night was actually illuminated by the eruption, an advantage to the Germans it was thought, on their nightly bombing raids on the port. One could see terrific fountains of flame and sparks, shot through with forked lightning and lasting for twenty minutes or more.

According to Curzio Malaparte in *The Skin,* the sea became blood-red and the whole horizon was 'plunged into an abyss of fire'; Neapolitans ran shrieking through the streets as houses rocked on foundations, while Allied soldiers 'wandered in bewilderment and terror' and Vesuvius 'screamed horribly in the red darkness'. All very surrealist and Goya-like. The sight of the eruption was thrilling but not a cause for panic.

A strong wind meant that the ash was fairly well dispersed, luckily for Nocera. An Allied airfield however was brought to a standstill. On the east slope of Vesuvius, at Turzigno, where the ash grains were up to an inch long, a British unit had to be evacuated because of a lava flow. Then when the rain started, the ground became so slippery with the wet ash that a convoy from Bari was halted.

Heavy rains invariably follow Vesuvius's eruptions. They had been responsible for the mudflow that submerged Herculaneum, by washing down accumulated

13. *Clearing the debris at San Giuseppe after the eruption of 1944.*

ash and debris. The great alarm now was about the fate of the 70th General Hospital, which was in the modern town of Pompeii and much closer to Vesuvius. Yet, as things turned out, it was less affected, again because of the wind.

During the afternoon of the 21st, several small earthquakes were felt at Nocera. Men were moved from wards on the upper floors. Parts of the hospital roof collapsed as the ash became heavier with the rain, and the dome of the church toppled over. However, there were no casualties. When it was ended, Vesuvius was still sprouting its enormous umbrella pine cloud.

As eruptions went, the last eruption of Vesuvius in modern times had been mild. There had not even been a mudflow. Bulldozers were brought to clear the mess at Nocera, but nothing could really be done about the ash, which had piled up to a foot and a half. 'For the next year it was like living in a coal-mine.'

Vesuvius had indeed been reduced slightly in height, but not as much as in 1906 when it had lost 325 feet. Now it is 3,900 feet high, but in Roman times it might have been 6,000 and once could have been up to 9,000.

Recent research has proved that there must have been a tremendous eruption about a thousand years before 79, with dust and ash falling in the direction of Avellino and Benevento. There are also traces of another much earlier eruption of at least equivalent intensity, again to the east. There is some speculation as to whether the top was literally blown off in 79, or whether half the crater's wall simply collapsed, leaving the other side intact; or whether either process began during the two ancient eruptions. In any case, after 79 a new, giant cone began to grow on the collapsed side, and it is this that is now properly known as Vesuvius. The old, truncated, dead cone is Monte Somma, so named after Summanus, the

14. *School building at San Sebastiano partly obliterated by lava, 1944.*

god of nocturnal lightning. A crater formed inside the Vesuvius cone, and it is in this that in normal times a small cone begins to build up.

The valley between Monte Somma and Vesuvius, fit for a Salvator Rosa landscape, is known as the Atrio del Cavallo. Here in the old days one left one's mount before the last struggle on foot through the clinkers up to the crater's mouth. Monte Somma protects the villages on the northern slope from the lava spills, though not from what are known as 'pseudo' lava flows, caused by the more violent fountains of liquid rock which leap up and over the rim – such a one devastated Ottaiano in 1779, as Sir William Hamilton recorded. In 1944 the largest spill – the one towards Massa – escaped round the corner of Monte Somma. Even farmers' walls can help to divert spills and, especially, mudflows. Thus in these days plans are ready for creating artificial barriers, especially by means of explosives, in cases of emergency, a technique successfully used with Etna's eruptions.

A theory that Pompeii in 79 was overwhelmed by a *nuée ardente,* similar to that which destroyed St Pierre in Martinique, has sometimes been discounted. Nevertheless, in the evidence of the skeletons at Boscoreale, nearer the mountain, and of those found during Murat's time at Pompeii, some feet above the first layer of pumice dust, it does seem that lethal gas must have been present in the first instance. Indeed even now fumes trapped beneath the deposits can be dangerous to excavators.

Volcanic eruptions are considered to be divided into five types: Peléan (after Mont Pelée in Martinique), Hawaian, Strombolian, Icelandic and Vulcanian, the last including the usual behaviour of Vesuvius. When there is a particularly violent Vulcanian eruption, it is sometimes called Plinian, after the famous descriptions of the 79 eruption that the younger Pliny wrote for Tacitus. The greatest eruption ever known in history, that of Krakatoa in 1883, when ash rose fifty miles and the explosion was heard three thousand miles away, was Plinian.

That summer I spent some time at Capo di Sorrento. The experience was a revelation to me. Even today, in spite of the high-rise buildings and polluted sea, I still regard the Bay of Naples and its surroundings as among the supreme beauties of the world.

I found myself in an Italy that exceeded my imaginings. It was far different to my miserable first impression when I landed from North Africa – and for that matter to the slit-trenches at Anzio. Every morning I used to swim in clear sapphire water among the ruins of a Roman villa, which I discovered had belonged to Pollius Felix and had been praised by Statius for its magnificence. In the late afternoons I would go further along the coast towards Sorrento, to another great ruined villa, where obviously every possible use had been made of natural features, including a bathing pool in a sea-water inlet and bridges to some

15. *The jumping pig; one of the treasures from the Villa of the Papyri.*

islands. There I used to watch the sunsets and the 'green ray' over Ischia. Then Vesuvius would turn mauve, and Naples looked like a string of diamonds.

Pollius Felix had another villa directly opposite at Pausilypon (Posillipo). Indeed Strabo said that the succession of houses and villas round the Bay made it seem as though the whole coast was one continuous town. There had been an imperial villa at Pausilypon, and Lucullus owned Megaris, where the Castel dell'Ovo now is. The younger Pliny owned six villas, while Cicero had three – at Pompeii, Cumae and Puteoli. We also now know that outside Herculaneum there was the sumptuous Villa of the Papyri, which was copied by the late Paul Getty for his museum at Malibu in California. There was the great domain, or ranch, at Boscoreale, owned by Publius Fannius Sinistor. The most fashionable spot of all was at Baiae, but the villas at Stabiae must have had some of the loveliest views.

It was not just the scenery, or the fertility of the land, that attracted rich Romans to the Bay. Naples, or Neapolis, was still an important centre of Hellenic ideas, regarded as essential to luxurious and civilized living. The library and bronzes (nearly all Greek or from Greek models) from the Villa of the Papyri are proof of the Romans' combined desire for comfort, beauty and cultivation of the intellect.

There were usually two types of villa: the peristyle, as at the Villa of the Mysteries and Sinistor's villa at Boscoreale, and the portico, which was more

16. *Fresco of a maritime villa from Stabiae.*

suited to the sea-edge, where houses could be built on several terraces and each room could command a view. One can get a very good idea of portico villas from the dream-like, rather Chinese paintings discovered at Stabiae.

I went to Capri and found that even there ash from the eruption was still a nuisance. At the time people had had to shake it off their pillows before getting into bed. Vesuvius from that distance looked so benign, so calmly majestic, so self-satisfied.

I also went again to Pompeii. By now I had grown to love the Neapolitan back alleys (strictly speaking out of bounds to Allied troops), and more than ever associated them with Pompeian street life. All that bargaining, yelling, pimping, thieving, singing, flaring of tempers must have gone on in exactly the same way in pre-79 Pompeii, and no doubt Pompeians also strung their laundry across the streets. Those piles of shining fish, luscious fruits and vegetables on counters along the alleys must have looked just the same at Pompeii. Then the contrast of plunging into those cool Neapolitan palaces, full of ornate furniture and guarded by black-eyed porters. Would there have been the same sense of unreality on entering the House of the Faun? Less furniture no doubt, and less stuffy. Did a visitor to Pompeii enter the Temple of Isis and find women like black bundles kneeling in prayer before a gilded goddess?

In 62 hardly a building at Pompeii escaped damage from the earthquake. Seneca said that many of the country villas were so badly damaged that they had to be abandoned. A flock of six hundred sheep had been swallowed in a chasm.

The rumblings underground had been terrifying. Out to sea there had been enormous waves. Then the reservoir had ruptured and there were floods. Nuceria was badly shaken, but the worst toll was at Herculaneum. No wonder, again according to Seneca, the experience sent some people out of their minds. Then, in 63, there was yet another bad earthquake.

A banker called Lucius Caecilius Jucundus, whose coarse-faced bust with remarkable ears is now in the Naples Museum, must have seen the column of the Temple of Jupiter crashing down in the Forum at Pompeii, for he had the scene commemorated on his *lararium*–the only pictorial record we have of that event. At the time Nero was making his début as an opera singer in Neapolis. He continued to sing as the building shook, nobody being allowed to leave the house until he was finished.

In spite of more tremors, the terrors of the earthquakes in 62–3 were soon forgotten, and reconstructions began at Pompeii and Herculaneum; so extensive at Pompeii that little was left of its Greek and Samnite origins. The Temple of Isis was magnificently rebuilt–it was one of the first major buildings to be disinterred in the eighteenth century. During this period the 'fourth' style of Pompeian wall decoration evolved, rather stage-like architectural fantasies, such as can be seen at the Houses of the Vettii and Castor and Pollux.

17. *Wall decorations in the* triclinium *at the House of the Vettii.*

18. *An eighteenth-century reconstruction of the Temple of Isis, Pompeii.*

Bulwer Lytton effectively drew on the younger Pliny's account of the eruption for the end of his novel. The inspiration for his scene in the amphitheatre presumably came from Dio Cassius' remark in the third century that the inhabitants were seated in the theatre at the time of the disaster, which was not actually the case. Dio Cassius also tells us that just before the eruption there had been subterranean rumblings 'like bellows'. If so, then the population must have already been in a state of nervous agitation. Springs had been drying up. 'Then suddenly a portentous crash was heard, as if the mountain were tumbling in ruins. First huge stones were hurled aloft, rising as high as the very summits; then came a great quantity of fine and endless smoke, so that the whole atmosphere was obscured, and the sun was entirely hidden, as if eclipsed. The day was turned into night and light into darkness.'

The day of the eruption was 24 August. Perhaps in that period of great heat rich people such as the family of Jucundus would have escaped to some cooler spot, as modern Neapolitans would now do. Because of Pliny's description, generally regarded as the first contribution to the science of volcanology, it is usually assumed that the explosion happened in the morning. Pliny was aged eighteen, but his account was written many years later, in the form of two letters to Tacitus, who wanted an eyewitness description for his history. He and his mother were staying in the house of his uncle and guardian, Pliny the Elder, then aged fifty-six, in charge of the Roman fleet at Misenum and regarded as one of the most learned men of the age, chiefly on account of his *Historia Naturalis.*

Young Pliny did not mention Pompeii and Herculaneum by name, though he spoke of a 'most beautiful country in ruins' and the destruction of 'so many populous cities'. For other places were lost too: Stabiae, Oplontis, Sora, Tora, Taurania, Cossa and Leucopetra. His uncle, he said, had been sunbathing that morning. After a light lunch the older man had gone back to his books, when young Pliny's mother asked him to look at a cloud of a very unusual shape and size. It is surprising that there is no mention in the account of the sound of an explosion. The time was one o'clock. 'My uncle immediately arose and went out upon a rising ground from whence he might get a better sight of this very uncommon appearance. A cloud, from which mountain was uncertain at this distance (though it was found afterwards to come from Mount Vesuvius), was ascending, the appearance of which I cannot give you a more exact description than by likening it to that of a pine tree, for it shot up to a great height in the form of a very tall trunk, which spread itself out at the top like branches – occasioned, I imagine, either by a sudden gust of air that impelled it, the force of which decreased as it advanced upwards, or the cloud itself being pressed back again by its own weight, expanded in the manner I have mentioned. It appeared sometimes bright and sometimes dark and spotted, according to whether it was more or less impregnated with earth and cinders. This phenomenon seemed to a man of such learning and research as my uncle extraordinary and worth further looking into. He ordered a light vessel to be got ready, and gave me leave, if I liked, to accompany him. I said I had rather go on with my work.'

As the uncle was about to set sail, he was handed a note from Rectina, the wife of Cascus. She wrote in the utmost alarm, 'for – her villa lying at the foot of Mount Vesuvius – there was no way of escape but by sea; she earnestly entreated him, therefore, to come to her assistance. He accordingly changed his first intention; and what he had begun for scientific reasons, he now carried out in a noble and generous spirit. He ordered the galleys to put to sea, and went himself on board with an intention of assisting not only Rectina, but several other people who lived in towns which lay thickly strewn along that beautiful coast. Hastening therefore to the place whence others had fled with the utmost terror, he steered his course direct to the point of danger, and with so much calmness and presence of mind as to be able to dictate his observations upon the progress and phenomena of that dreadful scene. He was now so close to the mountain that the cinders, which grew thicker and hotter the nearer he approached, fell into the ships, together with pumice-stones and black pieces of burning rock. There was now danger not only of running aground because of the sudden retreat of the sea, but from the vast fragments which rolled down from the mountain and obstructed the shore. He stopped to consider whether he should turn back again; but the pilot advised him: "Steer to where Pomponianus is. Fortune favours the brave."'

Pomponianus lived at Stabiae above the present Castellamare di Stabia. It would seem that Rectina must have lived near Herculaneum, so perhaps she had made her escape by the time Pliny neared her villa. As there is no mention of rain, the mudflow cannot have started, and in any case it has always been assumed that this would have begun about three days after the eruption. When Pliny reached Stabiae, he found Pomponianus already arranging to have his belongings loaded on to a ship. Unfortunately the wind was blowing inshore. 'My uncle embraced him tenderly, encouraging and urging him to keep up his spirits, and, thinking to soothe his fears by seeming unconcerned himself, ordered a bath to be got ready, and then, after having bathed, sat down to supper

19. The Destruction of Pompeii and Herculaneum *by John Martin, c. 1820.*

with great cheerfulness, or at least (which is no less heroic) with every appearance of it. Meanwhile broad flames shone out in several places from Mount Vesuvius, which the darkness of the night contributed to render still brighter and clearer. But my uncle, in order to soothe the apprehensions of his friend, assured him it was only the burning of the villages, which the country people had abandoned to the flames; after this he retired to rest, and it is certain that he was so little disquieted as to fall into a sound sleep: for his breathing, which, on account of his corpulence, was rather heavy and sonorous, was heard by the attendants outside. The court which led to his apartment was now almost filled with stones and ashes. If he had continued there any longer, it would have been impossible for him to have made his way out. So he was awoken and got up, and went to Pomponianus and the rest of his company, who had been feeling too anxious to think of going to bed. They consulted together whether it would be most prudent

to trust to the houses, which now rocked from side to side with frequent and violent concussions as though shaken from their very foundations, or make for the open countryside, where the pumice-stones and cinders, though still light, fell in large showers and were dangerous. In this choice they resolved for the latter: a resolution which for the rest of the company had been a choice of fear, but was taken by my uncle calmly and deliberately. So they went out, having pillows tied upon their heads with napkins; and this was their whole defence against the storm of stones that fell round them.'

Now it was day again, though to all intents they might have been in 'thickest night'. They decided to go down to the shore, but the waves were still extremely high. Pliny lay down on some sailcloth and called for cold water, which he drank. According to the account flames and whiffs of sulphur 'dispersed the rest of the party and obliged him to rise'. By flames he might have meant hot stones, unless it was a reference to lightning, which we know did strike Pompeii in several places during the eruption. 'He raised himself up with the assistance of two of his servants, and instantly fell down dead; suffocated, as I conjecture, by some gross and noxious vapour, having always had a weak throat, which was often inflamed. As soon as it was light again, which was not till the third day after this melancholy accident, his body was found entire, and without any marks of violence upon it, in the dress in which he fell, and looking more like a man asleep than dead.'

If Pliny really had succumbed to the gases, it is surprising that none of his companions were also affected. It is thought now that he might have had a heart-attack. And if Stabiae was eventually buried, how was it that his body was even recovered?

Presumably many Pompeians likewise found the waves too high to make their escape, for quantities of skeletons have been found at what was the sea-edge. Quite obviously the sooner the inhabitants left the threatened towns, the more likely they were to save themselves. Those who lingered because of their possessions, especially at Pompeii, were lost. It has been noticed that very few skeletons of horses have been found at Pompeii, which seems to show that some fortunate people managed to ride to safety.

Tacitus had been so interested in the account that he asked young Pliny to let him know what had happened meanwhile to his mother and himself. Young Pliny had said that in the evening he had gone to bed as usual, but there had been another earthquake, so violent that it 'not only shook but actually overturned, as it would seem, everything about us'. His mother rushed into his room and had found him in the act of getting up to awaken her. They went to sit on a terrace above the sea, and young Pliny took out his Livy to read. Here they were found by a Spanish friend of the uncle's who reproved them for being so unconcerned about the danger. 'Nevertheless I went on with my author,' said young Pliny smugly. Morning came, but the light was very faint. All around buildings were tottering, and it now became clear that they were in real peril. There then followed a scene fit for Malaparte's imagination. 'We resolved to quit the town. A panic-stricken crowd followed us, in dense array, driving us forward as we came out. At a convenient distance from the houses we halted, in the midst of a most dangerous and dreadful scene. The chariots, which we had ordered to be drawn out, were so agitated backwards and forwards, though upon flat ground, that we could not keep them steady, even by supporting them with large stones. The sea seemed to roll back upon itself, and to be driven from its banks by the convulsive motion of the earth; it is certain at least the shore was considerably enlarged, and several sea animals were left upon it. On the other side, a black and dreadful cloud, broken with rapid, zigzag flashes, revealed behind it variously shaped masses of flame: these last were like sheet-lightning, but much larger. . . .'

Malaparte, nearly 1900 years later, likened that black cloud to the ink-sac of an octopus, which is a good image, as Vesuvius sometimes does look rather like an octopus.

Young Pliny continued: '. . . our Spanish friend addressed himself to my mother and me with great energy and urgency: "If your brother, if your uncle, be safe, he certainly wishes you may be so too; but if he has perished, he would have wanted you both to have survived him. Why therefore delay your escape a single moment?" We could never think of our own safety, we said, while we were uncertain of his. Upon this our friend left us, and withdrew from the danger with the utmost precipitation.'

Again one detects self-congratulation. The ash cloud was beginning to descend. Already it had blotted out the island of Capri and the promontory of Misenum. 'My mother now besought, urged, even commanded me to make my escape which, as I was young, I might easily do; as for herself, she said, her age and corpulency rendered all attempts of that sort impossible—however she would willingly meet death if she could have the satisfaction of seeing that she was not the occasion of mine. But I absolutely refused to leave her, and, taking her by the hand, compelled her to go with me [towards Baiae?]. She complied with great reluctance, and not without many reproaches to herself for retarding my flight. The ashes now began to fall upon us, though in no great quantity. I looked back; a dense dark mist seemed to be following us, spreading itself over the country like a cloud. "Let us turn out of the high-road," I said, "while we can still see, for fear that, should we fall in the road, we should be pressed to death in the dark, by the crowds that are following us." We had scarcely sat down when night came upon us, not such as we have when the sky is cloudy, or when there is no moon, but that of a room when it is shut up, and all the lights put out. You could hear the shrieks of women, the screams of children, and the shouts of men; some calling for their children, others for their parents, others for their husbands, and seeking to

20. *Stage-set for the final act of Pacini's opera* The Last Days of Pompeii *at La Scala, 1827.*

recognise each other by the voices that replied; one lamenting his own fate, another that of his family; some wishing to die from the very fear of dying; some lifting their hands to the gods; but the greater part convinced that there were now no gods at all, and that the final endless night of which we have heard had come upon the world.'

There were all sorts of rumours—even that Misenum was on fire. Again there was mention of 'flames'. One burst 'fell a distance from us'. The ashes were so thick and heavy that every now and then one had to stand up and shake them off, 'otherwise we should have been crushed'. Young Pliny had really come to believe that it was the end of the world, and the thought that he was not dying alone somehow sustained him. 'At last this dreadful darkness was dissipated by degrees, like a cloud or smoke; the real day returned, and even the sun shone out, though with a lurid light, like when an eclipse is coming on. Every object that presented itself to our eyes (which were extremely weakened) seemed changed, being covered deep with ashes as if with snow. We returned to Misenum, where we refreshed ourselves as well as we could, and passed an anxious night between hope and fear; though, indeed, with a much larger share of the latter: for the earthquake still continued, while many frenzied persons ran up and down heightening their own and their friends' calamities by terrible predictions. However, my mother and I, notwithstanding the danger we had passed, and that which still threatened us, had no thoughts of leaving the place, till we could receive some news of my uncle.'

Pliny was writing for publication, and these two letters appeared in the six volumes of his collected letters. It is a pity that Tacitus' own version of the story has not survived.

Comparison between the 79 and 'Avellino' eruptions show that deposits from both were fairly similar, in that the lowest level is white pumice dust, followed by an abrupt change to greenish-grey which in turn is overlaid by dark or blackish ashes. It is considered that the climax of the eruption is indicated by the second layer of dust.

The results of the study of the Pompeii deposits show that the combined white and grey pumice reached a depth of 280 cm (110 inches) at Pompeii itself and 245 cm at Stabiae; at Pagani near Nuceria it was 180 cm and at Surrentum (Sorrento), because of the favourable wind, only 17 cm. Naples and Misenum would only have been affected by the ashes, as in the case of Nocera in 1944, and if any pumice fell on Herculaneum it would have been swept away by the mudflow. The amount of pumice grains that fell as a result of the less severe 1944 eruption was in comparison negligible.

The skeletons found during Murat's excavations in 1812 were twelve feet above ground level. Thus some people who had initially escaped the gases would have been wandering about over the pumice layer. When the 79 eruption was over, there was no trace whatsoever of Herculaneum. It had totally vanished. Some of the tops of Pompeii's taller buildings could still be seen, like masts today on the Goodwin Sands. Survivors and looters returned to dig. Was it then that someone, a Jew maybe, or a Christian, scratched the words SODOM GOMORA on a wall? Titus, who had only been emperor for six weeks, gave orders for some temple pictures and statues to be salvaged. Then plague and fire devastated Rome, and attention was diverted from Pompeii. In course of time topsoil and vegetation completely covered the town, so that all that was left was a large mound, known first as Civitas and then Civita. Meanwhile Resina grew up over Herculaneum. The Dark Ages descended upon Europe, and the elegant villas round the Bay were plundered and burnt. Gone were the bronzes and polychrome marbles of Pollius Felix. . . .

In about 91 Martial wrote a nostalgic epigram about Vesuvius's slopes, once the haunt of 'dancing satyrs' but now crowned by flames. Even the gods, he said, must mourn what they had done. This reference, and another by Galen, would seem to show that Vesuvius continued in a state of activity. Dio Cassius' account was the first to mention Pompeii and Herculaneum specifically by name after the eruption, but it was so fantastic that the Plinies would have been enraged. Before the eruption, he said, 'numbers of huge men', like giants, had appeared 'wandering over the earth day and night, and also flitting through the air'; later their shapes had been discerned in Vesuvius's smoke, to the sound of trumpets. He claimed that the ash had reached Rome, 'filling the air and darkening the sun', and had even been blown as far as Egypt and Syria.

Dio Cassius refers to an eruption in 203. The year 472 witnessed another, so great that ash on this occasion caused alarm in Constantinople. Other presumably paroxysmal eruptions occurred in 512, 685, 993 and 1036 – the first year in which a lava flow is recorded – and 1138.

There is no definite proof of a lava flow in 79. If there had been any then, it could easily have been buried by others in later years. The ejection of pumice dust and ash without lava flows means that the magma is becoming more acid, and from a geological point of view this usually indicates that a volcano is nearing the end of its life. Thus, on the assumption that there were no lava flows before 1036, that date is regarded as signalling a 'rejuvenation' of Vesuvius. Yet, according to Sir William Hamilton, there were no eruptions between 1139 and the murderous explosion of 1631 – which maybe is a happy precedent for present-day Neapolitans, Pompeians and Resinans, who might be encouraged therefore to expect no further eruption during their lifetimes.

After 1631 Vesuvius was in a continual state of activity, apart from the short rest periods, until 1944. In 1631 the eruption was again preceded by earthquakes and springs drying up. Animals, we are told, became restless the previous night, a common phenomenon before a major eruption or earthquake; birds disappeared. Then on 16 December there were explosions and thunderclaps. Ash and *lapilli* rained down, and it was like night. There were also lethal gases. Floods of lava rushed down at terrific speed to the sizzling sea. Then came the mudflows, which swept huge rocks before them. Herculaneum had another layer added to its covering. Portici and Torre del Greco were partly obliterated. The 'ink-sac' darkened the sky over Taranto. Once more records differ about the number of deaths; some say 4,000 died, others 18,000. Another piece of Monte Somma disappeared, and Vesuvius's crater was enlarged from one mile to three miles across.

As in the case of 79, those who fled at once survived. Those who waited died. The Spanish Viceroy caused a tablet to be put up at Portici, warning future generations of the evil and pitiless character of Vesuvius. 'As soon as an eruption begins,' he said, 'you must escape as quickly as you can. If you worry about your chattels, your greed and recklessness will be punished. Listen to the voice of this marble . . . flee without hesitation!'

Nearly sixteen centuries passed after the destruction of the towns beneath Vesuvius, and to all intents the names of Pompeii and Herculaneum had been forgotten. A few Renaissance scholars read their Pliny and Dio Cassius, and some wondered at the names on the road-maps of imperial Rome that continued to be used during the Middle Ages. The most famous of the Roman maps to have survived is the so-called Peutinger Table, now in Vienna; here quite clearly 'Herculanium' and 'Pompeis' are marked, with correct distances between them, though Oplontis was puzzlingly given even greater significance than either of them.

There had been excitement when a water channel had been dug through Civita and some marble fragments and coins had been discovered. In 1637 the German scholar Luc Holstenius visited the area and put forward the unfashionable view that Pompeii lay beneath Civita, not Stabiae as was generally supposed.

Milton went to Naples in 1638. Just over two hundred years later a visitor to the famous hermitage half-way up Vesuvius was told that there was a tradition that he had climbed the mountain several times. The account of his visits had been handed down from hermit to hermit. And it is true that Milton had left

21. *The hermitage on the slopes of Vesuvius, 1818.*

Rome in the company of a 'certain hermit'. Whilst in Naples he had been under the guidance of Manso, the biographer of Tasso. Manso in his book speaks not only of the 'gardens of Pompeii' but the 'smoke of burning Vesuvius'. So Milton must have been aware of the legendary lost town and probably also saw the volcano in eruption.

In 1689 there were more excavations for water at Civita; this time a slab was unearthed with the word Pompeii on it. However an academic row was simply precipitated by the discovery, Bianchetti the historian maintaining that at last proof had been found, Civita *was* Pompeii, and Pichetti the architect furiously denying it, the slab was merely something commemorating Pompey.

The seventeenth century ended with further speculation. For in 1699 Giuseppe Macrini published his *De Vesuvio,* in which he firmly pronounced that Pompeii was underneath Civita. He moreover claimed that he had visited the water excavations himself and had seen 'great halls' and houses. Even this book was treated with scepticism, and in due course the excavations were covered over and the vegetation grew again on the fertile volcanic soil.

II

DISCOVERY AND REAWAKENING

The dubious honour of initiating the excavations goes to a man with a resounding name: Emanuel-Maurice of Lorraine, Prince of Elbeuf and Duke of Guise. He came to Naples in 1707 in the service of the Emperor as commander of the cavalry.

Naples had been occupied by the Austrians in anticipation of the Treaty of Utrecht, when the Spanish inheritance was divided between Philip V and the Emperor Charles VI. For the previous two hundred years the Kingdom of Naples and Sicily had been ruled by Spain. The Austrians were not very welcome in Naples, and Vesuvius obligingly emphasized popular feeling by erupting during the vice-regal ceremonies. Ash rained down on the procession, the sky became dark, and there was a pine-shaped cloud.

Prince Elbeuf had a penchant for extravagant living and in 1710 decided to build himself a casino or small country house at Portici. About the same time a peasant dug a well in the vicinity and came upon a variety of costly marbles, which he thereupon sold to a local dealer. Elbeuf had imported a Frenchman who knew how to make a kind of cement from pulverized marble. When the Frenchman visited the dealer he was astonished by what he saw. He realized at once that the marble pieces must have been from an ancient building of importance.

Now the excitement began. Elbeuf bought the well and the surrounding land. Workmen were lowered into the cavity, about ninety feet deep, and made to dig horizontal channels underground. Some more interesting fragments were found. Then part of a statue of Hercules in Parian marble was brought to light. All splendid decorative material for the casino. Never mind the *mofeta,* the poisonous gases trapped underneath. The work must continue.

Elbeuf's 'greed' and totally unscientific methods of excavation have been reviled by archaeologists. Yet, secretly, most of us would rather sympathize with his enthusiasm, taking into account the age in which he lived. After more finds, an inscription was produced with the name of Appius Pulcher, a friend of Cicero and governor of Sicily. It was decided by Neapolitan scholars that Elbeuf had hit on a temple of Hercules. In actual fact it was the proscenium of Herculaneum's theatre. Then came the great sensation: three exceedingly beautiful draped female statues, considered at the time to be the Vestal Virgins, but now regarded as a mother and daughters.

22. *Dancer from the Villa of the Papyri.*

Elbeuf had meanwhile become engaged to a Neapolitan, the daughter of the Duke of Salza. As there was some official disapproval about this, he decided that it would be tactful to present these statues to his distinguished cousin, Prince Eugene of Savoy, who might also be instrumental in providing some much-needed cash. Then followed some complicated manœuvres. The statues had to be smuggled to Rome for restoration, then smuggled out (for Papal permission had to be obtained for the export of antiquities). They reached Vienna, and Eugene was predictably delighted. A special room was built for them and opened to the public.

Complaints from the Vatican reached the Austrian viceroy, and Elbeuf was warned to be more circumspect. Fewer treasures were forthcoming however, money was dwindling, and Elbeuf was frequently abroad. Thus the excavations seem to have ceased altogether in 1716. Elbeuf was promoted to field-marshal and transferred to France in 1719. Whatever he managed to take with him passed eventually to his heir, Charles IV of Lorraine, whose property was confiscated during the French Revolution. Nevertheless it is known that some objects from Herculaneum were left behind in the casino.

Vesuvius was very active during the next twenty years, which no doubt inhibited would-be excavators. In 1736 Eugene died and his art collection was immediately sold off by his niece. The three statues were bought by Frederick Augustus, King of Poland and Elector of Saxony (and are now to be seen at the Museum in Dresden).

There had been more jugglings with the map of Europe, and in 1734 a Spanish Bourbon, Charles, the eighteen-year-old son of Philip V, had found himself ruling the reunited kingdom of Naples and Sicily. Four years later he married Maria Amalia, Frederick Augustus' daughter.

The king was a keen huntsman and had acquired Elbeuf's casino as a lodge. Soon he decided to build a new royal residence at Portici, which would be his main country base until the palace at Caserta was ready. His queen of course had known the three statues well and initially it was partly thanks to her enthusiasm that, eruptions and earthquakes notwithstanding, excavations should have been resumed with such vigour. As the ground was so hard the king decided to employ a Spanish engineer, Joaquín de Alcubierre, another red rag to the archaeologists even if the years 1738–65 have been described as the 'heroic' period in the excavations.

It was decided to send down shafts blindly in the area around the peasant's well. Each shaft would be filled up as soon as it had served its purpose, so as not to endanger the foundations of the houses at Resina. Wherever possible gunpowder was used to speed the work. Nevertheless, astounding rewards were soon forthcoming: parts of two bronze horses, then jewellery and some statues, including one of Augustus. The erudite Marchese Venuti was lowered by rope

23. *A nineteenth-century Mexican visitor is shown the theatre at Herculaneum by torchlight.*

into the depths, and it was he who revealed that the theatre of Herculaneum had been discovered. The excavations thus went ahead with greater speed than ever. A prize find was the equestrian statue of Marcus Nonius Balbus, the most important man in Herculaneum; this was considered to be a greater work of art than the statue of Marcus Aurelius on the Capitol. Then a companion, Balbus' son, was found. It was realized that they stood outside the basilica or courthouse. Inside were busts of other members of the Balbus family, evidently a stern, highly intelligent lot, and three paintings: Hercules recognizing his son Telephus being suckled by a deer, Theseus triumphant over the Minotaur, the centaur Chiron instructing Achilles to play the lyre.

As it was still the fashion to repair antique statues, the work was entrusted to a Giuseppe Canart. Unfortunately the man was prone to melting down any bronze pieces which he felt were useless and turning them into commemorative medals of his own design. The pictures were also taken down from the walls and moved to the Portici palace, there to be covered with a veneer that was soon found to absorb some of the colouring. The king wanted the greatest secrecy to be kept. Nobody was allowed to do any sketching or to write about the discoveries.

However in November 1739 the site was visited by Charles de Brosses, with a permit arranged by Venuti. A full if rather prosaic account by this normally ebullient writer was sent to the Academy in Paris. Thus the news began to percolate through Europe.

The three frescoes caused the greatest interest, since so few paintings from Roman times had survived. They are still – especially the Hercules, which would appear to be derived from Pergamene statuary – regarded as among the most important to have been discovered, in either Herculaneum or Pompeii, excluding the frescoes from the Villa of the Mysteries and the Villa of Sinistor at Boscoreale. All the same, at the time some disappointment was expressed, and it was decided by artists that the pictures were merely 'weak reflections of lost masterpieces', though undoubtedly of enormous importance to antiquarians.

Six months after de Brosses's visit Horace Walpole and Thomas Gray arrived in Naples and were allowed to creep through the narrow passages at Herculaneum. 'This underground city is perhaps one of the noblest curiosities that ever has been discovered,' wrote Walpole to Richard West. They certainly did not find the place so nightmarish and oppressive as Dickens did a century later. Gray wrote to his mother how 'the passage they have made with all their turnings and windings is now more than a mile long. . . . As you walk you see parts of an amphitheatre, many houses adorned with marble columns encrusted with the same, the point of a temple, several arched vaults of rooms painted in fresco.'

24. *Telephus suckled by a deer: detail from a painting found at the Herculaneum basilica.*

All this was deep underground, by the light of smoking torches. Walpole spoke of architectural paintings and red backgrounds. Everything – statues, paintings, medals, gems, instruments of sacrifice, a table with lion's feet – was being removed for the king's pleasure. 'The wood and beams remain so perfect that you may see the grain!' said Gray. 'There is nothing of the kind known in the world,' said Walpole. Unhappily, he added, the work was 'under the direction of Spaniards, people of no taste or erudition, so that workmen dig as chance directs them, whenever they find the ground easiest to work'. Then again 'the people who show these antiquities are ill-tempered and very jealous'. Jealousy, personality clashes, close-fistedness and academic bumbledom were to bedevil the excavations for a large part of their history. And as Lady Mary Wortley Montagu said in 1740, 'They [the excavators] have broken it to pieces by digging irregularly.'

By 1745 it looked as though the treasures in the neighbourhood of the theatre and basilica were exhausted. By chance some objects had been dug up at Civita, still believed to be Stabiae, so on 1 April 1748 royal permission was granted to excavate on this new site. Mohammedan slaves, chained in pairs, were used to do the work. As it happened, excavating was also done at the real Stabiae, some miles further south, and famous frescoes were found there including *The Cupid Seller* and *The Flora*.

The work at Civita was of course much easier than at Herculaneum. Almost immediately there was some success – a fresco of garlands and fruit, a helmet, lamps and a skeleton of a man clutching some coins. Part of an amphitheatre was

25. *Galley-slaves excavating solidified mud near Herculaneum, c. 1780.*

26. The Cupid Seller, *one of the most popular of all the frescoes found beneath Vesuvius: a copy version by Tischbein.*

found. Alcubierre shifted to a new site, which turned out to be the building erroneously called Cicero's villa (near the Villa of Diomede). Here he unearthed the frescoes of the dancing bacchantes, centaurs and acrobats which were to cause such delight throughout Europe as soon as engravings of them were published. The frescoes were at once cut off the walls and taken to Portici, and the villa was in due course covered over again.

The only records of these discoveries were in Alcubierre's diary. Now he acquired an aide, a Swiss called Karl Weber, who was far more methodical. Indeed Weber was so careful, and so successful, that in consequence Alcubierre became jealous and actually sabotaged some of his work. However, just as it was decided that interesting finds at Civita were reaching an end, there came the sensational news of another discovery near Resina: the Villa of the Papyri.

This villa turned out to have a frontage of no less than two hundred and fifty metres. It had a belvedere, from which there must have been a superb view of the bay. Weber found that it consisted of an older smallish house with a peristyle, to which had been added a vast colonnaded area surrounding a garden and an oblong pool. In between each of the sixty-four pillars stood a piece of statuary, not only virtually undamaged but each of supreme artistic importance, some being original works of art and some copies of Greek masterpieces (in consequence of which contemporary artists again affected to be disappointed). Many of these statues and busts are famous the world over. They include the naked wrestlers, the drunken faun, 'Seneca', 'Sappho', the drunken Silenus, the sleeping satyr, Scipio Africanus, the two deer, the jumping pig, the five monumental dancers in Doric *peploi* and, above all, *Hermis in Repose*, a copy

27. Hermes in Repose, *an illustration from the* Anchità di Ercolano esposte, *Vol. III: one of the world's most famous statues and based upon an original by Lysippus (fourth century BC).*

from Lysippus. The famous and beautiful marble group of Pan copulating with a goat was also found here – the king considered it so shocking that he had it locked up at Caserta. Now it is the *pièce de résistance* in the 'Gabinetto Segreto', which houses the erotica at the Naples Museum.

The discovery of quantities of rolls of papyrus, approximately eighteen hundred in all, gave the villa its name and produced a possible clue as to its ownership. Needless to say the rolls were in a fragile state, and it took a long while for any to be unwound satisfactorily. There was much speculation about the possible results of the unwinding. At last, perhaps, the missing works of classical authors would be revealed. Eventually, it was discovered that the rolls were nearly all written in Greek. Then came an anti-climax. The first to be unwound was simply a ridiculous diatribe on music being harmful to morals. Most were the works of philosophers, and it was soon noticed that there were several, sometimes even duplicated, by the Epicurean Philodemus. Since Cicero had said that Philodemus was a friend of Lucius Calpurnius Piso, Julius Caesar's father-in-law, it was assumed that Piso and his descendants must have been the owners of the villa. Whoever they were, they appear to have been better judges of art than of literature.

28. *Design by James 'Athenian' Stuart for the Painted Room at Spencer House, London, 1759.*

The digging at the Villa of the Papyri continued until 1765. Weber died in 1763 but luckily for posterity he had made a detailed plan beforehand. Once again, the excavations were all covered over, even though part of the living quarters had not been explored. And there the situation rests to this day.

In 1748 Venuti published a description of the excavations to date, but it was immediately suppressed in Naples. However, an English translation appeared in 1750. Then in 1753 two Frenchmen, Cochin and Bellicard, published an account of their awesome experience of being guided by torchlight through the Herculaneum basilica, before the tunnels were refilled with rubble. As the king had now acquired the Farnese collection, his museum at Portici became legendary. Moreover, curiosity abroad about the new discoveries at Herculaneum became all the stronger when it was heard that there was still a restriction on sketching or taking notes. Restlessness also increased when it became known that the exclusive task of cataloguing the finds had been handed over to an old pedant, Monsignor Bajardi of Parma.

Robert Adam and Charles-Louis Clérisseau arrived in Naples in April 1755. It is strange to discover that they of all people should have apparently spent only a short while visiting Herculaneum and the Portici museum – but no doubt even that was considered a great favour. Adam wrote of his astonishment at seeing the

29. *Discovery of a skeleton at Pompeii; drawn by Fragonard.*

30. *The ithyphallic tripod found at Pompeii in 1755.*

papyri, paintings and mosaics. He also saw carbonized food and a 'chirurgical probe'. They saw 'earthen vases and marble pavements just discovered while we were on the spot'; and were shown 'some feet of tables in marble which were dug out the day before we were there'. The whole thing was 'exactly like a coal mine worked by galley-slaves who fill in the waste rooms they leave behind'. Indeed Adam seems only to have been modestly impressed by Naples. Clérisseau, however, recorded that he was able to make several drawings in the museum (which surely could only have been done through bribery) and presumably Adam was able to do the same.

The house of Julia Felix, with its frescoes of Egyptian gods and splendid peristyle of fluted columns and floral capitals, was brought to light that same year at Civita. It was here that a well-known folding table, with lions' feet topped by satyrs, was found. An inscription was also discovered to the effect that Julia Felix was the owner of ninety shops, all to let. Then the house was covered over. And on 15 June 1755 the famous ithyphallic tripod was discovered – three roguish satyrs holding up an incense burner or wash-stand.

31. *Robert Adam's design for the Etruscan room at 20 Portman Square, 1775.*

The king's enthusiasm could hardly now be checked, and at last he was convinced that Bajardi must be sacked. All Bajardi had done was to write five irrelevant tomes on the god Hercules, and to produce an exceedingly brief and uninformative catalogue without illustrations. The Academy of Herculaneum was thereupon founded with the express task of producing an illustrated description of all the main objects discovered, about 2,500 in all. Alas, almost immediately its distinguished members plunged into a welter of feuding and polemics. Finally Francesco Valletta took the matter in hand and was responsible for producing the first volume, published in 1757, of that seminal work in the later development of the Neo-classic movement, *Le Antichità di Ercolano esposte.*

The publication cost the king twelve thousand ducats. Six more volumes were to appear over the next twelve years, and a seventh in 1792. They were not for sale and were only given to those who had royal approval. The rivalry and competition for copies among European connoisseurs and scholars can be imagined. Not that the pictorial representations were all that exact – though to us they are imbued with a typically eighteenth-century charm and grace. To some contemporaries, who had welcomed the revival of interest in the art and philosophy of the ancient world as a return to purity and noble ideals, the 'depravity' of some engravings in volume VII – lamps in the form of phalluses, for instance – was a great shock.

The king had also founded the Capodimonte porcelain factory, which used several motifs from engravings in the *Antichità*. In 1759 he became Charles III of Spain, and the crown of the 'Two Sicilies' passed to his eight-year-old third son, Ferdinand. Charles left Naples with a great deal of regret, having given instructions that drawings of all major new discoveries at Herculaneum and Civita should be sent to him. The museum was left behind, absolutely intact, but, with a panache typical of a descendant of the Sun King, he removed the entire Capodimonte factory and re-established it at the Retiro in Madrid.

32. *A gladiator fights his own phallus.*

33. *Johann Joachim Winckelmann; etching by Angelica Kauffmann, 1767.*

Johann Joachim Winckelmann had been in Rome since 1755, the year in which he published his *Reflections on the Imitation of Greek Art*. His knowledge of antiquity was prodigious, his intellect formidable, his writing brilliant and visionary, and he was all the more remarkable in that period for being a self-made man. He came to Naples in February 1758. The very fact that his credentials and connections were so great made him an object of suspicion to the guardians of the excavations and the Portico museum. Indeed he found himself rebuffed and frustrated on every side, although he managed to obtain a copy of the *Antichità* volume. He had to give the usual undertaking not to make sketches in the museum and the satyr tripod was 'not available'. Greatly annoyed by this attitude, he took lodgings in a monastery near by. Still the excavations were denied to him. He found himself sidetracked to the study of methods of unwinding the papyri, in the charge of a Father Piaggi of the Vatican library.

He returned again in 1762, only to be confirmed in his impression that the excavating was being mismanaged and the whole business of cataloguing and preserving the discoveries a disgrace – greed was the prime motif behind whatever work was done, and Weber alone displayed any altruistic curiosity. The attitude in Naples was nothing less than an affront to scholarship. So he decided to launch into the attack and in that same year published a furious, deliberately insulting 'open letter' in his native German, to be followed by a supplement two years later. Copies of both documents were sent all over Europe to scholars and collectors, one of whom, Comte de Caylus, had the second translated into French.

A copy of this translation was given to Sir William Hamilton, as he left to take up his post as British envoy in Naples, to be passed on to Bernardo Tannucci, acting as regent during Ferdinand's minority. Inevitably a great storm broke, for most Neapolitan academics could not read German and had apparently hitherto been unaware of Winckelmann's tirades. Tannucci felt personally insulted. The fact that this coincided with important new excavations at Civita made the situation even more awkward for Winckelmann, who could hardly now expect to be welcome in Naples.

The early 1760s saw many important discoveries, including the paintings *Sappho* and *The Three Graces*, the Blue Vase, the tomb of Mamia and an inscription which finally proved that Civita was Pompeii. Then, at the end of the Street of the Tombs, a large fortified gateway (given the name of the Herculaneum Gate) had been found, showing that the entire town must stretch behind. The excitement among scholars was intense. Winckelmann was in due course forgiven and allowed complete access to the excavations; in return he agreed to review the latest volume of the *Antichità*.

Winckelmann's career ended in his ignominious murder in a Trieste hotel. He had done more than anyone else to make the world aware of the importance of

34. *Interior of the crater of Vesuvius, 1755.*

the excavations beneath Vesuvius. Some of his contemporaries violently opposed his adoration of the Greek ideal, but – as Hugh Honour has said – he was the poet and visionary of the Neo-classic movement.

Another death, that of Weber, just at the time of the discovery of Pompeii's real identity, was a considerable blow. His place was taken by Francisco La Vega, who initiated the habit of making plans of sites as they were excavated. But before long there were clashes with Tannucci. At least La Vega was able to put an end to the use of galley-slaves – 'cursed thieves' Samuel Sharp had called them in his *Letters from Italy* – obviously responsible for a great deal of pilfering. No doubt La Vega also took due note of one of Winckelmann's prize complaints about Alcubierre's régime: that when Latin inscriptions were found the bronze letters would simply be gathered up and thrown into a basket, without any effort at noting down their sequence.

The Temple of Isis was discovered in June 1765, another important milestone. The decorations and furniture were in an almost perfect state of preservation, and included the celebrated tripod of the winged sphinxes, holding up a basin decorated with garlanded ox skulls, that was to have such an influence on Empire

35. *The Tomb of Mamia, Pompeii, 1778–9.*

36. *The first discovery of the Temple of Isis in 1765; from Sir William Hamilton's* Campi Phlegraei.

design. On the altar of the Temple lay the bones of an animal that had just been sacrificed when Vesuvius erupted. A priest had attempted to hack his way out of a room with an axe. In another room the remains of a meal were found: carbonized fruit, eggs and nuts. There was also an inscription which proved the Temple had been entirely rebuilt after the 62 earthquake. A great mosaic was particularly admired. Indeed the very fact that the cult of Isis had been practised in Pompeii was a sensation in itself. Even the young, dim-witted king was persuaded to leave his hunting so that he could watch the rest of the excavating. And some decades later the temple provided inspiration for Bulwer Lytton (and thus indirectly for Madame Blavatsky).

Sir William Hamilton was present when the Temple of Isis was uncovered. He too was irritated by the slowness and muddle, still prevalent in spite of Winckelmann's efforts. The paintings from the Temple were all removed to Portici, where – so he said – they were simply confounded with the rest. He had arrived in Naples with the reputation of a connoisseur and man of taste. Almost immediately, his diplomatic duties not being too exacting, he began his famous collection of vases and other antiquities, some of which came from Pompeii and Herculaneum. Soon he prepared four lavish volumes, illustrating his collection and published by d'Hancarville. It was these that provided inspiration for Josiah Wedgwood's first vases when he opened his pottery works, known as Etruria, in 1769. They also served another purpose, for two years later his entire collection

37. *Inside the crater of Vesuvius, 1754.*

was bought by the British Museum for £8,400 by a special parliamentary grant.

Hamilton was also fascinated by Vesuvius, now more or less in a continual state of eruption. De Brosses had just missed the 1737 eruption, which had sent out a stream of lava a mile wide; he had vividly described the lava he had seen as frothing like red-hot milk on the boil. Adam had climbed the mountain in 1755 and has left his impressions in a letter to his mother: 'Though I had conceived a very horrible notion of it I assure you I was much disappointed to the better, as that great mouth, which is immensely deep and which sends out a pillar of flame and sulphurous smoke of an immense volume, exceeded much my conception, and from the growling thunder which every two or three minutes seemed to rise from the foundations of the hills surrounding the volcano, your ideas were converted into the most Hellish solemnity, whilst the view of nothing but sulphur, burnt rocks and ashes augmented the savage prospect.'

There had been another violent eruption in 1760, to the accompaniment of severe tremors, with a lava flow in the direction of Torre Annunziata. A new crater had formed on the side of the mountain. In 1765 James Boswell arrived in 'swarming, intense' Naples, eager to meet the 'great Hamilton'. He duly visited Portici and the ruins, and on 14 March (and possibly again on the 16th) he and John Wilkes climbed up Vesuvius, which proved to be a rather unpleasant experience. There was a great deal of sulphurous smoke. When they attempted to walk round the crater, they were almost suffocated and 'obliged to retire'. The descent was made with great difficulty, Boswell wrote in his journal, and sometimes they were 'almost up to the knees in ashes'.

Hamilton had first noticed a change in Vesuvius's behaviour in September that year. In 1766 he was elected a Fellow of the Royal Society in London. His graphic reports on Vesuvius's activity soon became famous in learned circles, and in 1772 they were published. This book (*Campi Phlegraei,* in two volumes)

Peintures Antiques d'Herculanum, Conservées dans le Museum de Portici.

38. *Two of the famous centaurs from the 'Villa of Cicero', Pompeii.*

39a. *Lava from the 1761 eruption cuts the road between Torre del Greco and Torre Annunziata; from* Campi Phlegraei.

39b. *Sir William Hamilton shows the king and queen the current of lava running down to Resina on the night of 11 May 1771.*

40. *Sir William
Hamilton*.

and another published four years later are regarded as pioneer works in modern volcanology. Walpole nicknamed him the 'Professor of Earthquakes'.

In November 1765 Hamilton climbed the snow-covered mountain. He noted that a little hillock of sulphur had been thrown up since his last visit. Whilst he was examining this, there was a report, and a column of black smoke, followed by a reddish flame shooting up 'with violence from the mouth of the volcano'. A shower of stones 'made me retire with some precipitation', and also 'made me more cautious of approaching too near, in my subsequent visits to Vesuvius'. And these visits were very numerous.

The main eruption began on 28 March the following year, with the usual shattering explosion, earthquake and fountain of translucent stones and cinders. The lava 'began to boil over the mouth' and just before there had been a black *pino* cloud. Typically Hamilton decided that not only must he climb the mountain again but that he would spend the whole night up there. The lava was running at the rate of a mile an hour.

'I approached the mouth of the volcano,' he wrote, 'as near as I could with prudence; the lava had the appearance of a river of red-hot and liquid metal, such as we see in the glass-houses, on which were large floating cinders, half-lighted, and rolling one over another with great precipitation down the side of the mountain, forming a most beautiful and uncommon cascade. The colour of the fire was much paler and more light the first night than the subsequent nights, when it became of a deep red, probably owing to its having been more impregnated with sulphur at first than afterwards. In the day-time, unless you are quite close, the lava has no appearance of fire, but a thick white smoke marks its course.'

On the 31st he decided to spend another night up there, this time taking with him Frederick Hervey, the future 'Earl Bishop'. He thought things were going to be safer, as the 'perfectly transparent' red-hot stones, weighing up to fourteen pounds each, were shooting off in the opposite direction. He underestimated the situation. As Hervey told his daughter: 'At last, after about an hour's fatigue, we reached the summit, where we found a great hollow of almost forty feet and half a mile round: at the bottom of this were two large mouths from whence the mountain frequently threw up two or three hundred red-hot stones some as big as your head, and some considerably larger. One of these struck me on the right arm, and without giving me much pain at the time made a wound almost two inches deep, tore my coat all to shreds, and by a great effusion of blood alarmed my companions more than myself. In a few days it became very painfull, then dangerous, and so continued to confine me to my bed and my room for near five weeks.'

There followed a quiet period for Vesuvius, so Hamilton made his nephew Charles Greville join him on an expedition into the crater to collect salts. Suddenly they heard the 'most dreadful inward grumblings, rattling of stones, and hissing', and had to escape pretty smartly. In October 1767 Vesuvius burst forth once more with so much vigour that the king and Tannucci had to escape from Portici at two o'clock in the morning. The lava only just missed the royal palace and museum. Vineyards were destroyed. For a whole week there was a 'perpetual scene of horror'. 'The streets of Naples have been full of processions attended by women with bare feet and hair loose.' Prisoners rioted and the archbishop's gatehouse was set on fire because he refused to bring out the relics of the city's patron saint, San Gennaro.

Needless to say, Hamilton felt he must climb up again, in spite of shaking earth and volleys of stones. 'The explosions from the top of the mountain were much louder than any thunder I ever heard and the smell of sulphur was very offensive.' The guide became alarmed and 'took to his heels'. Hamilton wisely followed suit. 'I was apprehensive of a fresh mouth, which might have cut off our retreat. I also feared that the violent explosions would detach some of the rocks off the mountain of Somma, under which we were obliged to pass.' The pumice-stones were 'like hail', so he decided to return to his villa, 'where I found my family in great alarm at the continual and violent explosion of the volcano which shook our house to its very foundations, the doors and windows swinging on their hinges'.

From Naples the mountain was completely obscured by dense clouds, out of

41. *The Large Theatre, Pompeii, 1793, by J. P. Hackert.*

which there issued continual flashes of forked or zigzag lightning, and the sun appeared 'as through a thick London fog or smoaked glass'. People were obliged to carry umbrellas to keep off the ashes. 'We were in expectation every moment of some dire calamity.' There was such a panic in the city that the king arranged for a procession of twenty thousand people to march to the nearest point of Naples to Vesuvius. San Gennaro was invoked, and to the satisfaction of all Vesuvius was 'calm'd' and the lava ceased to run.

Ferdinand had officially come of age in 1767. He enjoyed mixing with low company, and thus became popular among the *lazzaroni* of Naples who nicknamed him *Nasone* (Big Nose). As for the excavations, he found them inexpressibly boring and could hardly be persuaded to pay attention to their progress. The following year he married Maria Carolina, a daughter of Maria Theresa of Austria and considerably more intelligent than he was. When her brother, Emperor Joseph II, visited Naples, it was considered that Hamilton would be by far the most suitable person to conduct him round Pompeii.

42. *Vien's interpretation of* The Cupid Seller *against an elegant Neo-classic background.*

Hamilton obliged, and his eloquence was such that even the king's interest was momentarily stirred. The Large Theatre had just been discovered. La Vega also carefully arranged for some objects to be left in a prepared spot, so that they could be unearthed, as though for the first time, in the presence of the imperial visitor (a ruse that was to persist for the next half century). Joseph was suspicious, but nevertheless so enthusiastic that he endeavoured to impress on Ferdinand that some sort of patronage for the excavations was necessary. At least he did succeed in making his sister interested.

Soon Hamilton found himself 'in the character of the best cicerone in Naples'. In 1776, for instance, he had to conduct Duke Albert of Saxony and the Archduchess Maria Christina round the ruins, and in 1782 he escorted the Grand Duke Paul and his wife.

A less august visitor, though a lively writer, was Lady Anne Miller, whose book on Italy was published in 1776. She visited the 'Cabinet' at Portici but complained that it was still the case that 'no person who visits [it] is permitted to take away any sketch, note or memorandum on the spot'. The equestrian Balbi were preserved in glass cases, she said, but the mosaics were all laid on the floor for you to walk over. She claimed that eleven bronze statues from the Herculaneum theatre had been melted down and turned into coins.

Henry Swinburne, author of *Travels in the Two Sicilies,* arrived a little later, and like Lady Anne was excited by the collection of domestic and everyday things at the museum – 'lamps in endless variety, vases and basins of noble dimensions, chandeliers of the most beautiful shape, pateras and other appurtenances of sacrifice, looking-glasses of polished metal … a kitchen completely fitted up … specimens of various sorts of eatables, retaining their shape though burnt to a cinder'. To which catalogue she had added musical instruments, goblets, phials, medals and cameos. Swinburne saw the Temple of Isis, which he described as a 'small, neat sanctuary, not a grand fabric'; there were 'disagreeable vacancies', he said, where the paintings had been cut out of the walls. It was also strange to see cultivated land around the excavations. He noticed the root of a vine just above where the statue of the goddess had been.

It is not surprising to learn from his book that the excavations were still being

43. *Entrance to Pompeii,* c. 1778.

carried on 'as hope or caprice actuated the minds of the engineers'. He also added: 'A very small number of workmen is now employed in uncovering this curious city; the reasons given for such slackness are a satiety of antiquities, and the difficulty of finding proper spots to lay the rubbish upon: the king is obliged to take a lease of the land he chooses to open, and must also have ground to deposit the earth taken out.'

The budding musician Michael Kelly arrived in 1779. He described how he climbed Vesuvius and, on the way up, talked to the hermit, who turned out to be French and had once been a hairdresser in London. Again the mountain was in a 'villainous humour, emitting flames and large bodies of lava'. And, sure enough, in August there was another tremendous eruption, which 'will be remembered all their lives by all who chanced to be in Naples at that period'. For days the scene was 'appalling'. There were 'horror and dismay in every countenance, and despair in every heart'.

A fissure had already opened on the north-east side of Vesuvius and lava had been flowing from it throughout June. The eventual explosion came to be known

44. *Robert Adam's design for a chair for the Etruscan dressing-room at Osterley, 1776.*

as the 'centenary eruption', since it occurred almost exactly 1,700 years after the disaster of 79. According to Hamilton this time there was a liquid fountain of fire two miles high, and it was this that turned into a 'pseudo' lava flow in the direction of the unfortunate Ottaiano. 'The sight of the place was dismal,' wrote Hamilton, 'half buried under black *scoria* and dust, all windows towards the mountain broken, some of the houses burnt, the street choaked with ashes–in some narrow streets to a depth of four feet, so that roads had to be cut by people to reach their own doors. During the tempestuous flow of ashes, *scoria,* and stones, so large as to weigh a hundred pounds, the inhabitants dared not stir out – even with the vain protection of pillows, tables, wine casks, etc. on their heads. Driven back wounded or terrified, they retreated to cellars and arches, half stifled with heat and dust and sulphur, and blinded by volcanic lightning – through twenty-five minutes the horror lasted; then suddenly ceased, and the people took the opportunity of quitting the country, after leaving the sick and bedridden in the churches. One more hour of this frightful visitation and Ottaiano would have been a buried city like Pompeii.'

It is to be hoped that the roofs of Ottaiano's churches did not collapse. In Naples, according to Kelly, the panic was so great that the majestic figure of Father Rocco had to step in, for he had the 'most unbounded power over the lower orders'. The *lazzaroni* had been demanding that the archbishop should carry the statue of San Gennaro up the mountain, but the archbishop 'thinking discretion the better part of valour', had escaped to Capua. So it was up to Father Rocco to command the *lazzaroni* to disperse, which they did, and soon afterwards Vesuvius obligingly quietened down, to remain in a period of repose for five years.

When William Beckford arrived in November 1780 to stay with the Hamiltons, he was overcome with a strange mixture of sensations on seeing the effect of the 'mischiefs of the late eruption' on the 'most luxuriant and delightful scenery of nature'. The gladiators' barracks at Pompeii had been among the more recent discoveries, and these he inspected. Whilst at the Temple of Isis he fell into a reverie, and wrote in his diary how he imagined the people of AD 79 rushing about in a frenzy while long-robed priests desperately made sacrifices in the hope that their goddess would intervene. All in all, his romantic mind had been thrown into a 'melancholy, not disagreeable, tone'.

Tannucci had been responsible for a more systematic approach to the excavations. Instead of the haphazard diggings of the past he had directed La Vega to work towards the centre of the city from the Herculaneum Gate. Debris had to be removed outside the town, which of course meant that the actual progress was slower. The queen supported La Vega in his feud with Tannucci, and in 1777 Tannucci was sacked, which only resulted in the work becoming more lackadaisical than ever. Visitors complained that odd bits from different statues were stuck together, and that every object was treated simply as an accession of wealth for the Royal family and not as a thing of intrinsic interest or beauty. They also found themselves treated as potential thieves, which is not perhaps surprising as a black market in Pompeiana was thriving in Rome. We read, for instance, of Lady Holland bringing back a bust of Caligula from Herculaneum as a present for Walpole.

The 1779 eruption resulted in ash falling once more on Pompeii. There was also alarm lest the Portici museum might some day be overwhelmed. Thus it was decided to remove some of the main treasures to the present building in Naples, recently vacated by the Jesuits, and this was done with great fanfare.

Goethe had studied Winckelmann's works, which had partly inspired him to visit the South of Italy. He arrived in Naples in February 1787, accompanied by the artist Tischbein. Hackert, the landscapist, took them to call on Hamilton (in that year partly responsible for reviving the Herculaneum Academy) to find that 'after many years of devotion to the arts and the study of nature' he had now discovered the 'acme of those delights' in the person of a twenty-year-old English girl, Emma Hart, who undeniably had a beautiful face and figure. This Emma had originally been Greville's mistress, but Hamilton was besotted by her. He

45. *Excavations at Pompeii, c. 1793, by J. P. Hackert.*

46. *Treasures from Herculaneum and Pompeii brought in procession to the Naples museum; the king and queen are in the box at the left.*

would make her let down her hair and put on flowing Grecian dresses, and she would then strike 'attitudes' in the manner of the Herculaneum dancers – sometimes standing in a large gilt frame. Goethe could hardly believe his eyes. 'It is a performance like nothing you have ever seen.' They were also shown Hamilton's secret treasure vault. A lid from a chest was lifted and there were two magnificent candelabra, which they assumed had 'found their way' from Pompeii.

The two distinguished visitors went to Pompeii on 11 March. Like others they were impressed by its smallness and compactness; the houses they thought were like architects' models or dolls' houses (the Houses of the Vettii and the Faun, etc. were of course yet to be discovered). 'This mummified city,' Goethe said, 'left us with rather a disagreeable impression', but his spirits revived as his party sat in the vine-covered pergola of a small inn and watched the glittering sea.

Yet he found himself haunted by the memory of the place, and two days later returned. 'Many a calamity has happened in the world, but never one that has caused so much entertainment to posterity as this one.' It was on that day, at sunset, that he sat by Mamia's tomb and again admired the view of the sea.

Then to the Herculaneum theatre and the Portici museum, denuded though it was of some of its prizes. Now, Goethe said, his idea of Pompeian life had

47. *The colonnaded court of the Gladiators' Barracks near the Large Theatre, Pompeii, 1792.*

changed. The houses in one way must have looked cramped, because they had been so full of objects, but they were also spacious, because these very things were so beautifully made that they 'enlarged and refreshed the mind' – something that even the largest room could not do. He also – chauvinistically, though with justification – regretted that the theatre had not been excavated by Germans, instead of being 'casually ransacked' as if by brigands.

Goethe was one of the first to have guessed – correctly – that the ashes and dust must have hovered in the air above Pompeii before descending on it. Vesuvius also intrigued him. He went up on 2 March, and noted that the lava flow of 1771 was already covered with a thin moss. He also inspected another flow only five days old. After a while he found breathing difficult. The smoke then became so thick that he could not even see his shoes. So he turned back. On the 6th he decided to try again. Tischbein was reluctant to accompany him – as an artist he found the lava 'shapeless', not to say depressing, since it was constantly destroying itself and therefore 'declaring war on beauty'. He was no happier when he saw the stones shooting out of the crater. Goethe, on the other hand, felt an urge to defy the danger, something which he knew was illogical, for the sight was 'neither instructive nor pleasing'. As he stood on the edge of the 'monstrous abyss', the whole mountain shook and a 'terrific charge flew past us'. Yet even a rain of ashes did not frighten him away, and he continued with his methodical examination of the lava.

On the 20th he heard that there had been a new lava flow on the far side of the mountain, so up he went again, determined to reach the source itself, which he succeeded in doing. He was completely reckless. When he saw a huge cloud of steam, he went straight up to it. The ground became 'hotter and hotter' and a 'whirl of dense fumes' was almost suffocating. At one time the guide had to grab him and force him back. Vesuvius was a 'peak of hell', he declared, and stood 'in

48. *Lady Hamilton in a classical attitude; by Richard Cosway, 1800.*

the midst of paradise'. Then on his return, he saw a magnificent sunset. Again that contrast. And yet 'the Terrible beside the Beautiful, the Beautiful beside the Terrible, cancel one another and produce a feeling of indifference'. He also added: 'The Neapolitan would certainly be a different creature if he did not find himself wedged between God and the Devil.'

When Goethe departed for Rome, after visiting Sicily, Tischbein stayed behind in Naples. He became very friendly with Hamilton, who arranged for him to publish four volumes illustrating his second collection of vases 'discovered in sepulchres in the Kingdom of the Two Sicilies'. Once more these books were to have a considerable effect on Josiah Wedgwood's designs; they also had an influence on Flaxman and Fuseli.

In 1791 Hamilton, in the words of Walpole, 'actually married his Gallery of Statues', i.e. Emma, when it would appear that she immediately began to put on weight (though this did not prevent her from continuing with her 'attitudes'). Meanwhile the Bastille had fallen, and Louis XVI and Marie-Antoinette, Maria Carolina's sister, had been imprisoned. Tension and alarm grew in Naples, and in 1793 a French fleet made a show of strength in the Bay. Then the French king was executed, and France declared war on Britain. A treaty was signed between

49. *The cone of Vesuvius, 1832.*

50. *An eruption of Vesuvius painted by Joseph Wright of Derby on his return from Italy in 1775.*

Britain and the Two Sicilies. Hamilton then found himself in a position of unusually hectic diplomatic activity.

On 11 September, Captain Horatio Nelson, on board the *Agamemnon* reported his first sight of Vesuvius. He was made very welcome by the king and at once became friendly with Hamilton, though it seems unlikely that he saw much of Emma on this occasion. Shortly afterwards news arrived that Marie-Antoinette had also been guillotined. 'I shall pursue my vengeance to the grave,' wrote the frantic Maria Carolina under her sister's picture in her room. In the atmosphere of gloom even less attention was paid to Herculaneum and Pompeii, where a few convicts performed some desultory digging. Then in June 1794 Vesuvius chose to make one of its paroxysmal eruptions.

If Hamilton had had little time recently for ruined cities, he could not be kept away from this eruption, which he believed to be one of the most violent ever recorded. There was the usual earthquake beforehand, but so severe that it had caused alarm at Caserta and was felt at Benevento. Three days later there was a great spray of fire from the mountain, and Hamilton counted fifteen separate

51. *Lava invades Torre del Greco, 15 June 1794.*

torrents of lava. There were 'horrid' noises, like heavy artillery, accompanied by a continuous hollow murmur 'like that of the roaring of the ocean during a violent storm'. Next came enormous clouds of black smoke with the customary zigzag flashes. Then a great stream of lava, originating from six separate *bocche,* poured through the main street of Torre del Greco and continued 362 feet into the sea. Like the elder Pliny, Hamilton approached the scene by boat. When he put his hand into the water it was scalded. Soon his boatman 'observed that the pitch from the bottom of the boat was melting fast and floating on the surface of the sea, and that the boat began to leak'. So they 'retired hastily' and landed 'at some distance from the hot lava'.

The scene at Torre del Greco was one of incredible desolation. The cathedral was covered by forty feet of lava, though the average depth was thought to be twelve feet. Some of the timbers of houses were still burning. Yet only fifteen people out of a population of eighteen hundred had died.

Meanwhile in Naples there had been complete darkness day and night, and the weight of ash had made roofs collapse. This time the archbishop was induced to carry a phial of San Gennaro's blood through the streets.

When all was over it was seen that Vesuvius had completely altered shape and was now lower than the ridge of Monte Somma. Mudflows had caused great damage to vineyards and farmland. Hamilton, now in his mid-sixties, struggled once more through the fine ash up to the crater. He saw that several smaller craters had formed, and reported that by the end of his visit the soles of his shoes had been burnt completely through.

In 1798 the French entered Rome and drove out the Pope. That was the year of the Battle of the Nile, and of Nelson's triumphant return to Naples, when his famous *ménage à trois* with the Hamiltons began. Ferdinand sent an army to the north, but it was ignominiously defeated, and as a result Nelson had to evacuate the Royal family and the Hamiltons to Palermo. The king and queen took some small objects and coins, considered to be of special value, from the museum. Hamilton sent his collection of vases back to England on the *Colossus*. He was shattered when he heard that the ship had been wrecked off the Scillies.

Nearly 180 years later, in 1975, the British Museum acquired the remnants of the *Colossus'* cargo after it had been raised by frogmen. Thanks to Tischbein's drawings it has been possible to piece some of the vases together.

III

THE ROMANTICS

We shall have to skip over the French occupation of Naples, and the great advances in the excavations at Pompeii under Championnet, Joseph Bonaparte and, especially, the Murats, when more was done than in the whole previous half century. Space also makes it impossible to digress on the effect of the *Antichità* volumes on Neo-classic and Empire taste, or to examine the work of Adam and his followers, or of Clérisseau, David, Canova, Ermandshoff, Thomas Hope, Thorvaldsen and others. It is enough to say that in decoration, as distinct from other arts, the influence of Pompeii and Herculaneum only became really pronounced at the end of the eighteenth century, and that it was especially apparent in Germany between the 1820s and 1830s, the outstanding names then being Leo von Klenze and Karl Friedrich Schinkel. Ludwig I of Bavaria

52. *Plate from the Etruscan Dinner Service made at Capodimonte for George III, c. 1790.*

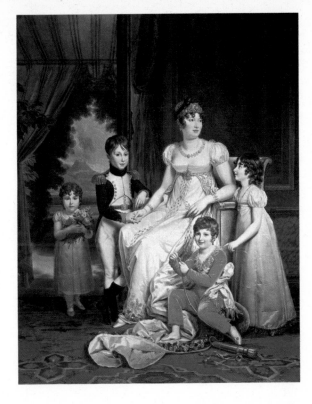

53. *Queen Caroline Murat
and her children.*

commissioned a copy of the House of Castor and Pollux at Aschaffenburg on the
River Main. Later, in Paris, Prince Plon-Plon created an elaborate *palais
pompéien* on the Avenue Montaigne. And in Palermo, starting in 1867, the
Politeama Garibaldi was erected in the Pompeian style, with a pretty little
bandstand (also Pompeian) opposite, put there by the Whitakers, English
marsala wine merchants, to protect their view.

The French occupation also attracted writers to the ruins, such as
Châteaubriand, Madame de Staël, Stendhal and Lamartine, in whose novel
Graziella there are celebrated descriptions of Pompeii and Vesuvius,
supplemented later in his *Mémoires inédites*. After 1815 the British flocked to
Naples, and Sir William Gell, a genial bachelor, became Hamilton's successor as
the most favoured and expert cicerone. Gell's *Pompeiana*, a delightfully
illustrated guidebook, appeared between 1817 and 1819 and was a very great
success, being the first work of its kind to appear in English. Geologists like
Humboldt, Davy and Lyell climbed Vesuvius, with important results for volcanic
theory.

There is an amusing account by Lady Morgan, in 1821, of her struggling up to
the crater, only to find a group of English dandies 'laughing, flirting and
chattering' over the bubbling lava – most provoking after having travelled so far
and enduring such fatigue, 'in the hope of a new sensation, that of meeting
Nature alone and sublime'. By then Romanticism was reaching its zenith, and
Shelley wrote two letters to Thomas Love Peacock about visits to Vesuvius and

54. Le Joueur de flûte *in Prince Plon-Plon's Pompeian House, 1860; Gautier is standing in the centre.*

Pompeii. He watched the sunset from the volcano, the effect of its flames making the scene even more beautiful. He decided to climb into the crater by torchlight, only to be overcome by the fumes, so that he had to be supported back to the hermitage on the slopes below. He was astonished by Pompeii and by the 'ideal life' represented in the paintings. 'It seems as if, from the atmosphere of mental beauty which surrounded them, every human being caught a splendour not its own.' Then there was the glorious scenery all around. Pompeians had been able to 'contemplate the clouds and lamps of heaven; could see the moon rise high behind Vesuvius, and the sun set in the sea, tremulous with an atmosphere of golden vapour, between Inarime [Ischia] and Misenum'. Every now and then he and his companions heard the 'subterranean thunder' of Vesuvius. They found the Street of the Tombs the most impressive thing of all. Along the broad stones 'you hear the late leaves of autumn shiver and rustle in the stream of the inconstant wind, as it were, like the step of ghosts'. Afterwards they sat on a lava rock by the sea. Shelley's 'expressive countenance was languid, despondent, melancholy, quite sad'. Obviously it was then that inspiration came for the 'stanzas written in dejection' in his *Ode to Naples,* actually completed in 1820

near Pisa after he had heard of a Neapolitan insurrection, and echoing his letter
to Peacock:

> *I stood within the city disinterred;*
>   *And heard the autumnal leaves like light footfalls*
> *Of spirits passing through the streets; and heard*
>   *The Mountain's slumberous voice at intervals*
> *Thrill the roofless halls;*
>   *The oracular thunder penetrating shook*
> *The listening soul in my suspended blood;*
>   *I felt that Earth out of her deep heart spoke –*
> *I felt, but heard not: – through white columns glowed*
>   *The isle-sustaining Ocean-flood,*
> *A place of light between two heavens of azure.*

Edward Bulwer Lytton came to Naples in 1834 from Rome, where he had been
writing *Rienzi*. It is said that Antonio Bonucci, La Vega's successor, spotted him

55. *Sir William
    Gell.*

56. *The Street of the Tombs, Pompeii, 1837; by Samuel Palmer.*

sitting disconsolately on a stone bench and engaged him in conversation, out of which emerged *The Last Days of Pompeii*. It has also been suggested that Lady Blessington gave him the idea for his plot. Certainly Gell provided him with much of the material for the very authentic picture he gives of first-century Roman life. According to Lytton's son, some inspiration derived from a picture of the last days at the Brera gallery in Milan. All the same, the theme was by no means new. Macaulay, Schiller, Delphine Gay and Joseph Méry had written poems on it, and there had been an opera at a Scala on the subject in 1828. Compared to *Graziella,* Lytton's book is full of skippable passages for the present-day reader, not to mention appalling sentimentalities. Yet the basic story is brilliant and the ending a superb contrivance – when the blind flower girl, as the only person in Pompeii who can find her way without seeing, guides the man she loves and his betrothed through the rain of ashes to safety.

There were counter-reactions to the enthusiasm that followed its publication. Dr Arnold, for instance, simply saw the whole Bay of Naples as a 'fearful drama of Pleasure, Sin and Death' – Death being manifest in the 'awfulness' of Vesuvius. If Pope Pio Nono was prepared to deliver a blessing from the Temple of Jupiter, Maximilian of Mexico saw nothing grand or sublime about Pompeii.

57. *Madame de Staël as Corinne, 1808–9; by Mme Vigée-Lebrun.*

To him it was an 'indiscreet' glimpse of Roman life. 'The little rooms still glitter in glaring colours, like painted corpses.'

Maximilian's trip to Vesuvius seems to have been more enjoyable, however much the lava presented a 'charmless picture of horror' and the colours in the crater were crude and 'lacking in freshness'. He felt 'alone amongst all the terrors of nature, in this eternally stirring desert'. Eggs were boiled in the steam, and stones were hurled into the depths, 'producing a sort of thunder'. Then came the descent, 'the famous gliding through the ashes'. 'It was undeniably agreeable.'

58. *Edward Bulwer Lytton.*

59. *A page from the first edition of Gell's* Pompeiana.

The whole company was like a herd of he-goats, 'capering, half dead with laughing, flying, running, jumping'. At last they reached a spot where 'Naples, amidst the light and green, washed by the laughing sea, lay in full splendour at our feet, before our enraptured eyes'.

There had been another minor eruption of Vesuvius in 1845, to inaugurate the new Observatory it was said, but too soon for Professor Luigi Palmieri's renowned seismograph (still to be seen there) to provide warnings. The Observatory stood on high ground, two thousand feet up, in a situation where lava could safely flow on either side. Thus Palmieri, that 'intrepid soldier of science', was able to remain at his post during many subsequent eruptions, including the paroxysmal one of 1872. The eruption of 1850 was particularly severe, and in 1855 it was feared that a lava flow might even reach Naples. Other large lava flows occurred in 1858 and 1861, after which Vesuvius decided to slumber for a short while, in preparation for 1872.

The excavations at Herculaneum had been resumed in 1828, not by means of subterranean passages but *all'aperto*, leaving buildings exposed. Yet they had proved somewhat disappointing, and in 1855 they were once more abandoned. As for Pompeii, when Prince Pückler Muskau visited it, he mockingly said that there were only thirty workmen on the site, fifteen children and fifteen mules – and this in spite of the sensational unearthing of the House of the Faun, which contained not only the Alexander mosaic, considered still to be one of the most outstanding mosaics of the ancient world yet discovered, but the bronze of the Dancing Faun itself, on a par with those found at the Villa of the Papyri. But Ferdinand II, 'King Bomba', had enough political worries on his mind.

60. *A view of Pompeii from the first edition of* Pompeiana.

We must also pass over Leopardi's poem *La ginestra,* Baudelaire's *Le Jeune enchanteur,* Herman Melville's visit and the important though sometimes ponderous tomes on the ruins by German historians and archaeologists. In 1860 Garibaldi entered Naples, where he was joined by his old friend Dumas *père,* who had been writing enthusiastic war reports on the Sicilian campaign. As a reward Garibaldi not only installed him at the Palazzo Chiatamone, but made him director of the excavations and the museum.

It goes without saying that Dumas was thrilled. He would invite French scholars to help him. The glorious days of the Charles III and the Murats would

return . . . However, there was considerable annoyance among the Neapolitans about the appointment of this bearded, theatrical foreigner, and stories circulated about public money being wasted on orgies at the Palazzo. After all, the point of the Risorgimento was to give Italy to the Italians. One day Maxime du Camp called on Dumas, to find him with his head bowed over a table on which were spread plans of Pompeii. As usual Dumas was full of enthusiasm. '*Hic jacet felicitas*', he misquoted the sign mentioned by Gautier over the shop that sold golden priapuses. Suddenly a mob appeared outside and there were shouts of 'Away with Dumas! To the sea with Dumas! *Fuori straniero!*'

61. *Vesuvius in eruption, 1817; by J. M. W. Turner*

62. *The House of Actaeon, from* Pompeiana.

Hungarian troops had to be called out to protect him. Dumas could not believe it, his eyes filled with tears. 'I was accustomed to the ingratitude of France,' he said, 'but I did not expect that of Italy.' Nevertheless he remained in Naples for four more years.

His books continued to pour out, and meanwhile he tried, unsuccessfully, to open a restaurant. The main achievement of his régime had been an appropriate one: the cataloguing and checking of the 206 pieces of erotica in the Gabinetto Segreto, many of which had never hitherto appeared in any inventory.

IV

SYSTEM, SCIENCE AND METHOD

The man chosen by the new king, Victor Emmanuel II of Savoy, to take over the direction of the excavations was Giuseppe Fiorelli, and no better choice could have been made. Fiorelli was aged thirty-seven and had been in prison under the Bourbons, during which time he had written a history of Pompeii. Some years before he had also made his mark in exposing an archaeological fraud at Cumae. Since Victor Emmanuel was anxious to obtain as much publicity and international recognition as possible for the new Italy of the Risorgimento, he gave Fiorelli every encouragement. So by January 1861 no less than 512 men were working at Pompeii.

The arrival of Fiorelli is regarded as the real beginning of systematic and scientific excavations. He published a journal recording all new finds, their exact positions and any conclusions drawn. Rubble was removed outside the city, not left in inconvenient dumps. He arranged for important buildings to be protected, and devised the *insulae* system whereby the whole of Pompeii was divided into sections and the houses numbered. Workers were carefully screened for honesty. Above all, he arranged – as far as possible – for objects and paintings to be left where they were found, and not removed to Naples. Then, as mentioned earlier, he invented the system of filling the cavities left by bodies with plaster of Paris.

When the king visited Pompeii in 1869, he was so pleased with Fiorelli's work that he gave him a personal donation of the then great sum of 30,000 lire. Fiorelli decided to use this money for recommencing excavations at Herculaneum.

It was under Fiorelli's direction that the *lupanar* or brothel was discovered, next door to the inn of Sittius – convenient no doubt for clients. The walls of each cell were painted with copulating couples, either for titillation or so that you could choose your preferred position – the room downstairs appears to have been for those who did not care about privacy. Another find was a bakery with no less than eighty loaves in an airtight oven.

The gaily irreverent Mark Twain came to Pompeii in 1867. The cart ruts made him indignant. The Street Commissioners, he said, could not have been doing their job and the taxpayers had been swindled. When he saw his first skeleton he was saddened, until he realized that it might have been that of a Street Commissioner. After visiting Pompeii, Baiae and Rome he came to this conclusion:

'Men lived long lives in the olden time, and struggled feverishly through them, toiling like slaves, in oratory, in generalship, or in literature, and then laid them down and died, happy in the possession of an enduring history and a deathless name. Well, twenty little centuries flutter away, and what is left of these things? A crazy inscription on a block of stone, which snuffy antiquaries bother about and tangle up and make nothing out of but a bare name (which they spell wrong) – no history, no tradition, no poetry – nothing that can give it even a passing interest. The thought saddens me.'

He had also of course climbed Vesuvius, over lava flows like 'a black ocean tumbled into a thousand fantastic shapes'. It was difficult, he said, to believe that this 'far-stretching waste of blackness, with its thrilling suggestiveness of life, of action, of boiling, singing, furious motion, was petrified!' The edge of the crater was like a huge circus ring. No fire was visible but one could smell the whiffs of sulphur that issued 'silently and invisibly from a thousand cracks and fissures'.

In 1871 Professor Palmieri's seismograph began to be disturbed. Then early in the morning of 12 April a large discharge of incandescent 'projectiles' came showering down, killing a number of medical students who were climbing the mountain. Next the entire cone split, and lava poured down the Atrio del Cavallo through the Observatory Gap, above which the professor was bravely perched, and through the unfortunate villages of Massa and San Sebastiano. Although all in all there was not a great loss of life, it was reckoned that this was one of the

63. *Bakery at Pompeii; a tinted photograph that belonged to Fiorelli.*

64. *The Pompeian Room in the Garden Pavilion at Buckingham Palace.*

greatest eruptions in Vesuvius's history, and without any doubt the end of a cycle. The smoke and ashes had probably reached five thousand feet above the cone.

The new cycle that followed, lasting until 1906, was carefully studied. After a two-year repose period cone-building and lava flows began in the crater. By 1881 the crater was nearly full, and there was an overflow of lava, forming a kind of cupola, dubbed Colle Margherita after the Queen of Italy. Similarly another cone near the Observatory came to be called Colle Umberto after the king. By the end of 1905 Vesuvius had risen to 4,338 feet above sea-level.

In 1875 it was decided once more to abandon work at Herculaneum as houses at Resina were being threatened with collapse. In any case results had again been less spectacular than hoped for. By and large the nineteenth-century work at Herculaneum had been confined to what are now known as Insulae II and VII, including the House of Argo.

65. In the Temple *by Alma-Tadema, 1871, with an exact representation of the sphinx tripod found in the Temple of Isis.*

At Pompeii in that year, however, there had been an important find: a box containing a quantity of wax tablets detailing the business transactions of Caecilius Jucundus. Also in 1875 Fiorelli was promoted to Rome as director of all museums and excavations in Italy. His place was taken first by Michele Ruggiero and then by Giulio di Petra.

The excavations proceeded apace, marvel after marvel was revealed. Houses were often named after visiting royalties. Sometimes they were called after specific incidents, like the House of the Centenary, excavated in 1879, eighteen hundred years after the eruption – it was here that an attractive bronze satyr and the only fresco actually depicting Vesuvius were revealed. The House of the Silver Wedding was so called in 1893 in honour of the king's and queen's anniversary; after the House of the Faun it is the grandest and most luxurious in Pompeii, with well-preserved frescoes of the 'second' style. Then in 1896 the House of the Vettii was found.

The seven-volume work by Roux Ainé on the bronzes and paintings of

Herculaneum and Pompeii (1875) was one of the last of the old-style illustrated publications. As usual many of the line engravings were adapted from the *Antichità*, but with a typically Late Victorian flavour. Murray's *Handbook for Southern Italy* came out in 1855, to be followed by Baedeker's in 1861: both landmarks in tourism. Dyer's *Guide to Pompeii* was published in 1875, for the more capacious pocket. In 1883 Augustus Hare's *Cities of Southern Italy and Sicily* appeared. His caustic comments are still worth reading, viz:

Portici 'All guides here are imposters, and should be rejected.'

Vesuvius 'Delicate persons, who do not wish to make the final ascent of Vesuvius, will find it quite worth while to drive as far as the Observatory, for the sake of a near view of the lava streams. . . . Everyone should wear their worst clothes; boots are ruined by the sharp lava, and coloured dresses are stained by the fumes of the sulphur.'

Pompeii 'The first impression on entering the mummied city is always one of disappointment . . . The windowless houses . . . look more like ruined cow-sheds or pig-sties than anything else . . . A winter of the nineteenth century would be unendurable in the comfortless toy houses of Pompeii.'

On leaving the Museum 'Wearied with filthy streets and dirty yelping people, let us now turn from the Museum up the hill . . .'

The collection of Herculaneum paintings '. . . nothing exceptional compared to

66. *The ascent of Vesuvius, mid nineteenth century.*

masterpieces mentioned by classical authors, but such as it is, it is a most precious deposit of ancient art, full of variety and beauty, of simplicity and truth, and of knowledge of form and colour.'

This last comment on the paintings is just the impression that Renoir seems to have had when he went to the Naples museum in the winter of 1881. He records that he copied many of the frescoes. 'You have no idea how restful it was for me, when I arrived in this town, full of the art of Pompeii and the Egyptians – those priestesses [the bacchantes?] in grey-green tunics seemed just like the nymphs of Corot.' It was cold, so at Pompeii he painted a great deal out of doors, to be warmed by the sun. Thus he found himself concentrating on 'the great harmonies' instead of bothering about small details which 'obscure the sun instead of inflaming it'.

Another distinguished visitor who came repeatedly to Pompeii towards the end of the century was the Empress Elizabeth of Austria. In 1896 she had bronze casts made of the Herculaneum wrestlers for her Achilleion at Corfu.

In fiction *Gradiva* (1904) by the German Wilhelm Jensen might be mentioned,

67. *The House of the Hunt, 1889; the* tablinium, *with traces of fourth style decoration and vignettes of hunting scenes.*

68. *Silver cup found at Boscoreale; now in the Louvre.*

though not because it is important literature. A form of ghost story, it concerns the obsession of a man with the foot of a girl on a Pompeian bas-relief, which turns into flesh and blood. The unfortunate author soon found his book under close critical scrutiny, on the score of fetishism, unconscious erotic drive and repression, by none other than Sigmund Freud.

A dramatic discovery occurred at Boscoreale in 1895. Fiorelli had made some preliminary investigations on the site of a *villa rustica,* a self-supporting farm on the slopes of Vesuvius just over a mile from Pompeii. There had been difficulties with the owner of the place, so work had been abandoned. But a new owner decided to excavate on his own account, as a result of which an enormous cache of wonderfully executed silverware and quantities of gold coins was found. This man kept his discovery secret and managed to smuggle the treasure to Paris. There it was bought by Baron Edouard de Rothschild, who presented most of it to the Louvre.

The farm had obviously been a place of great luxury and contentment, and death must have come very swiftly. The watchdog was still on its chain, and the horses were still in the stable. Evidently the people who hid the treasure in the wall were suddenly overcome by fumes and had toppled down on it – giving a certain point to its two most celebrated pieces, a pair of flagons decorated with skeletons, meant to be an exhortation to enjoy life while time remains.

Other villas were found near by, one at Boscotrecase being found to have belonged to Agrippa Postumus, the grandson of Augustus, and containing a slave-barracks, with cells for offenders. At Boscoreale two other large houses were discovered, Publius Fannius Sinistor's and another belonging to Lucius Herennius Florus. The room known as the Aphrodite Hall in the former's house contained an important series of paintings, mostly of figures with strange, meaningful stares, which along with other items are now scattered in Amsterdam, New York, Paris, Naples and elsewhere.

These new finds had the effect of reviving interest in the excavations generally, and in Herculaneum in particular, thanks to the energy of Charles Waldstein,

69. *Excavating the House of the Vettii.*

70. *The family of Obellius Firmus. The two on the left are holding hands; at their feet are two children with arms entwined.*

Reader in Classical Archaeology at Cambridge and, from 1904, Director of the American School of Classical Studies in Athens. It was his conviction that important works of art must still be buried at Herculaneum, more important than most of the things so far found at Pompeii. He also believed that, given the fact that it was so much more difficult and therefore expensive to dig through the solidified mud, all civilized countries should contribute towards the costs. He argued that Pompeii had been pre-eminently a commercial town, and that its artistic influences had been primarily Italic; Herculaneum had been more culturally inclined and the discoveries there had indicated a distinct taste for Greek art, of a higher artistic quality. Nothing from Pompeii, he said, more strikingly conveyed the distinctive characteristics of Greek mastery than the two Herculaneum paintings on marble, 'Latona and the Knuckle-Players' and the 'Centauromachia'. He launched his project for an international organization in 1903, and succeeded in obtaining the backing of Edward VII. The plan was to secure the help of the richest men in the world, under the leadership of the king and government of Italy. Following a series of false rumours and bureaucratic blunders, the Italians began to take umbrage and felt that their prestige would be damaged. Then, just as Waldstein was on his way to approach Pierpont Morgan, the whole affair was scotched, and excavations at Herculaneum were again postponed.

In 1906 Vesuvius once more took the limelight, for in April there was another prodigious eruption, as a result of which the mountain lost over 300 feet. Lava *bocche* opened up, one only 1,800 feet above sea-level. Blocks of old lava, incandescent *scoriae* and cinders were ejected high into the sky, some falling back into the crater. There were lurid lightning flashes and a huge pine-tree cloud. Part of Torre Annunziata was again covered with lava. Then, as had occurred in 1779, *scoriae* and rocks were shot over the ridge of Monte Somma towards Ottaiano. In a church at San Giuseppe 105 people were killed when the roof collapsed on them. The final drama took place at 3.30 a.m. on 8 April, and lasted for about fifteen hours, during which time the cone was blown off – a truly alarming sight. The funicular railway, built originally by Thomas Cook, which had survived many previous eruptions, was (for the first time) wiped out. One feature of this eruption was the building up of ash banks which subsequently developed into

71. *House of the Vettii; fresco in the fourth style in the* lararium *depicting domestic spirits and the guardian serpent.*

72. *Wall decoration from the Villa of Diomede; drawn in 1825.*

'hot avalanches'. There was also some very heavy rain, resulting in disastrous mudflows, especially in the direction of Ottaiano.

Vesuvius was quiet for the next seven years. Then, as usual, the crater began to fill up. There were some eruptions and lava flows, finally ending in the last paroxysmal explosion of March 1944.

From 1905 to 1910 the excavations were in the charge of A. Sogliano, and from 1910 to 1924 under V. Spinazzola. As a result of the vast amount of new discoveries at the turn of the century, it became easier to formulate the four styles of Pompeian decoration. The first or incrustation style was considered to date from 150 to 80 BC. This was mainly in imitation of marble, but also included small architectural features. Examples of this style can be seen at the Houses of Sallust and the Faun. The second or architectural style occupied most of the rest of the first century BC. Probably based on stage scenery, it was intended to give the illusion of depth and space, some of the best examples being in the Houses of the Silver Wedding, the Labyrinth and the Cryptoporticus – there is also a superb set of second style wall-paintings from Boscoreale at the Metropolitan Museum in New York. Pastoral scenes, still-lifes, foliage and mythical or religious compositions, including the Dionysiac figures at the Villa of the Mysteries, were also painted at this period.

The third or Egyptian style lasted until just before the year of the earthquake. This was a reaction away from bold architectural designs to frail columns or bronzes adorned with minute decorative details. Miniature landscapes on central

73. *Asellina's* Thermopolium *where hot and cold drinks were served.*

points of walls were also painted at this period, this time perhaps in imitation of tapestries, which would have had such scenes woven into them as panels. The House of Lucretius Fronto provides one example of this type of decoration. Aspects of the third style seem to have especially attracted Robert Adam.

With the fourth or ornamental style we are back to architecture, but more fantastic and blatantly theatrical. This 'decadence' covers the period from about AD 55 to 79, during the time of reconstruction and derived one imagines from Neronian Rome; a good example is seen at the House of Castor and Pollux. A great variety of other types of painting was also going on at this time, however, best seen at the House of the Vettii, which was completely decorated during those last seventeen years.

The *Nuovi Scavi,* or new excavations, date from Spinazzola's régime. These roughly speaking, cover the Street of Abundance, Pompeii's main thoroughfare, lined with shops and stretching from the Forum to the Sarnus Gate, and all the buildings to the south as far as the town walls. The appointment of Amedeo Maiuri in 1924 marked the beginning of another great period in the history of Pompeii's resurrection. It is to him that we owe the policy of attempting to re-create the atmosphere of buildings' interiors by leaving domestic utensils *in situ* and restoring walls and ceilings. Three shops worth singling out are those of Verecundus the clothier, with a folk-art mural of a Venus being drawn by four elephants, Verus the blacksmith and Stephanus the fuller, whose job it was to wash and thicken cloth.

Many of Maiuri's finds are described in his attractive books of discursive essays, *Passeggiate campane*. They include accounts of the Thermopolium, where not only were drinks available, but also, one suspects, the ladies whose names appear on the walls: Aegle, Maria, Smyrna and Asellina; the major part of the House of the Mysteries; the House of Menander, with its marvellous collection of silver, mostly Hellenic and equalling that of Boscoreale; the House of the Cryptoporticus, containing many pathetic huddled bodies, including a woman with a girl's head buried in her bosom.

In 1926 Waldstein, by now Sir Charles Walston, came to Maiuri to discuss

74. *A cast of a corpse in the museum at Pompeii.*

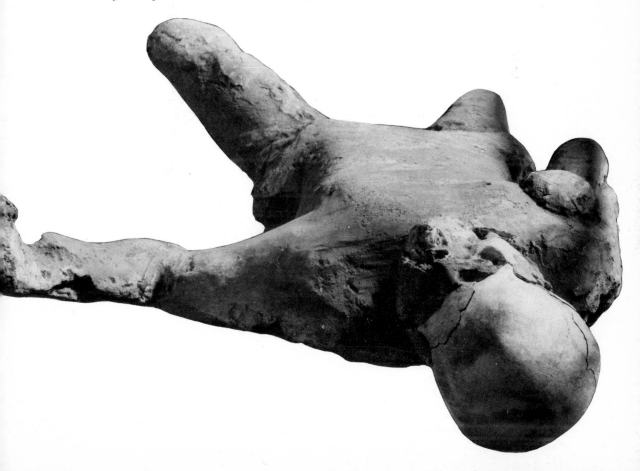

75. *One of a pair in the House of the Stags, Herculaneum; a gruesome but outstanding piece of animal sculpture.*

once more the question of digging up Herculaneum. At last he was successful, but unfortunately he died the following year, only a few months before the excavations started. In recognition of his efforts his ashes were buried in an urn found in the town.

Over the next years, the three areas known as Insulae III, IV and V were mostly uncovered, with spectacular success. Walston had been right: Herculaneum had been a more elegant place to live in than Pompeii, probably with a population of less than five thousand. There were fewer shops, and it was noticeable that there were no cart ruts in the streets and no stepping-stones over them. Then – as remarked upon earlier – woodwork had been preserved by the mud. Upper storeys were also sometimes intact.

The town of Resina prevented – and still does – excavations on the north-eastern side, towards Vesuvius. It is a curious sensation now to walk in the empty streets, among these grand houses of the past, and to look up at the jumble of gardens and cheap modern buildings, on the very verge of the cliffs of mud. Maiuri worked in a systematic way, which makes for another contrast, when one sees the tunnels – admittedly very impressive – of the Bourbons.

76. *'The Arch of Nero', Pompeii; by Luigi Bazzani, 1895.*

77. *Between the Large and Small Theatres, Pompeii.*

Again the policy was to leave paintings and mosaics undisturbed, even if they were of high quality. The House of the Deer was one of the most important discoveries, with a depth of 130 feet and containing the two well-known groups of deer being attacked by dogs – the most outstanding pieces of animal sculpture found at either Herculaneum or Pompeii – and the statues of the satyr with the wineskin and the 'vigorously indelicate' drunken Hercules. Other buildings excavated by Maiuri at the time included the Samnite House, with an upper gallery and resembling in some ways a palace of the Renaissance; the House of the Mosaic Atrium and the House of the Wooden Partition, the most completely preserved private house to have survived, again either at Herculaneum or Pompeii.

The people of Herculaneum may have been richer than the Pompeians but this did not make them any the more reticent about matters of sex. No brothel has come to light there, but plenty of phalluses have been found. The House of the Deer has an enormous mural of a naked woman being clasped by a bronzed male (while a ram wanders by unconcernedly). There is a very crude phallic drawing on the wall of the wine-shop, and in the House of the Gem we read: 'The Emperor Titus' doctor Apollinaris had a good shit here'. We also learn that Apelles the waiter had fun with Dexter, the slave of Caesar, in a back room of the Suburban Baths.

The area known as Insula Orientalis II was the next to be excavated, and it is this that includes the House of the Gem, the House of the Relief of Telephus (still only partly unearthed and probably belonging to Balbus) and the Suburban Baths, beautifully preserved and containing outstanding stucco work.

At Pompeii one of the major tasks begun before the Second World War was the clearing of the Palaestra or sports ground, next to the ampitheatre. This area, 450 feet square, was surrounded by a portico. In the centre there was a large swimming pool, surrounded by rows of plane trees. About a hundred skeletons were found here, including those of several youths who had evidently taken refuge in the latrine. Here Professor della Corte, author of many works on Pompeii, discovered the puzzling anagram on a pillar at the Palaestra:

ROTAS
OPERA
TENET
AREPO
SATOR

Because of the word TENET, repeated in the form of a cross, some think the anagram has a Christian significance, but the stumbling block to its interpretation has always been the apparently meaningless AREPO. Actually it must have been widely known in the Latin-speaking world, for an identical inscription, scratched on a tile, was found in 1868 at Cirencester in England.

There has also been speculation about a mark, as of a cross wrenched off, above a wooden piece of furniture, very like a *prie-dieu,* in a little room in the House of the Bicentenary at Herculaneum. Could this have been to do with a Christian slave? Whatever its true interpretation, there is indeed something strangely moving about the place.

V

HERCULANEUM AND OPLONTIS

In 1940 Mussolini entertained the German Minister of Education among the red-painted columns of the House of Menander. That same year he entered the war, and in 1943 the Allies invaded Sicily. On 9 September 1943 the Allies landed at Salerno. The main treasures in the Naples museums had already been crated up. Immediately 187 cases were despatched for safety to the monastery of Monte Cassino: twenty-seven containing large bronzes; sixty with small bronzes; fifty-one containing paintings; and three cases from Capodimonte.

Luckily, as it turned out, the infamous Hermann Goering Division decided that it must protect this treasure from 'Anglo-American barbarians' and they were removed to the divisional headquarters at Spoleto. The Italians were suspicious, and some five months passed before the cases were transferred – with much sanctimonious fanfare on the part of the Germans – to the Vatican. That appeared to be the situation, as far as the Neapolitan authorities were concerned, when I reached Naples in February 1944.

After the Allies had reached Rome, it was realized that eighteen of the cases had disappeared. These had contained all the Pompeian gold and jewellery, the two bronze deer from the Villa of the Papyri, an Apollo, a dancer from the Papyri and the *Hermes in Repose*. Then it was revealed that they had all been taken to Berlin in December 1943 as a birthday present for Goering.

But the cases had been removed once more, to a salt-mine at Alt Aussee. Here, in May 1945, they were discovered by American troops, taken to Munich and then returned to Naples. Thus they escaped the fate of the contents of the Filangieri museum – which included paintings, ceramics, enamels and ivories – and the nine hundred cases from the Neapolitan State Archives, which had been stored near Nola and methodically and totally destroyed by the Germans.

Herculaneum suffered some blast damage. The worst losses at Pompeii from bombs were at the Houses of the Moralist, Sallust and the Faun, which lost its *atrium* and five rooms, including frescoes of the first and fourth style. Part of the Pompeii museum was totally lost. However, the bombs did at least lay bare two new sites: the Villa of the Marine Gate and the Temple of Dionysus. It was fortunate for both towns that the main battle swept round the north side of Vesuvius.

78. *Two bronze deer from the Villa of the Papyri.*

There is a legend that an American airman dropped a bomb into the crater, which precipitated the eruption in 1944. It is of course perfectly possible that there was such a bomb, and this could well have disturbed the cone. But no major eruption would thereby have been caused. There was some small activity as early as November 1941, which Professor Imbo of the Observatory attributed to the cone being 'crumbled' by a bomb–which might have been the one in question.

Pompeii can still astonish, but not in the same way as it did travellers in pre-Lytton days. It is no longer 'veiled by the mind's dark imaginings', which Rose Macaulay has said is the true pleasure of ruins. Visit it early in the morning, one is advised, so as to avoid the crowds. Wise counsel, but even so it is hard to find that quiet corner for indulging in a Beckford-like reverie.

Yet those carefully prepared, numbered sites, all divided into regions and *insulae,* with padlocks on doors and entrance fees, are not supposed to contain riddles: quite the contrary. The charm of Pompeii and of Herculaneum, to go back again to Rose Macaulay, is that of looking as through a telescope at a remote age incredibly brought close to us, 'a bright, unfaded miniature, clear and eerie like a dream'. The classical past is made familiar to us, and yet remains distant.

When Haruko Ichikawa, author of *Japanese Lady in Europe,* trailed round Pompeii with a group of tourists, she remarked on the 'nonchalant air' of her companions while the guide spoke of Vesuvius. 'Only we citizens of Tokyo, with Mount Fuji near us, secretly counted our fingers, thinking how many years had elapsed . . .' And she added: 'I can bear to be buried somehow, but it would not be very pleasant to become part of a show excavated after two thousand years.' With which most of us would uneasily agree.

Pompeii might almost seem to have become an industry, and this no doubt is why it features so seldom nowadays in imaginative literature, and merits only brief mentions in travel books. Roger Peyrefitte wrote a notable story in defence of the often maligned guides. After all, he pointed out, they are also custodians – we don't want any more graffiti scribbled on the Forum walls. They

79. *Herculaneum today, showing the houses of Resina above.*

80. *Pallas Athene advancing with spear; marble statue from the Villa of the Papyri, probably a direct copy of an archaic Greek original.*

are, moreover, often the victims of tourists' meanness. Malcolm Lowry's splendid story *Present Estate of Pompeii* contains the often quoted phrase about the *lupanara* being made for a race of voluptuous dwarfs. To be frank, he did not like Pompeii. 'The traveller has worked long hours and exchanged good money for this. And what is this? It is some great ruin that brings upon you the migraine of alienation . . . It is as if you could hear your own real life plunging to its doom.' More recently, in 1970, Henry Reed's dramatic poem *The Streets of Pompeii* was performed with music on the BBC. Beckford would probably have approved of much of it, the emphasis being on the essential ghostliness of the place: the Dancing Faun snapping eternal fingers in drunken bliss; the statue of the sad

81. *Bronze serpent with five heads that stands in the centre of the still partly excavated swimming-pool in the Palaestra, Herculaneum.*

gaunt woman in the Street of the Tombs, with an expression of somebody trying to remember; whispering slaves in the Villa of the Mysteries; the statues in the House of the Vettii looking as if they were for sale . . . And if you had an aerial pick and shovel, and dug far enough into the sky, would you in the end find the tops of all those broken houses?

As for films, the last to date was made in 1949 by the French director, Marcel l'Herbier. There have in fact been several. The first on record was produced by Arturo Ambrosio and directed by Luigi Maggi. Italians had turned to this and other classics because they were out of copyright – a reaction to the infringement case resulting from Zecca's film version of *Quo Vadis* in 1901. The second was apparently made by the same producer in 1913, with Mario Cesarini directing. In 1926 a third major version appeared, again from an Italian studio, this time directed by Amleto Palermi, his co-director being Carmine Fallone, who later became one of the most prominent Italian directors of spectaculars.

The subject certainly seems to be crying out for the 'Sensurround' treatment.

Excavations at Pompeii began again in 1951, in particular along the town walls, among the nearer suburbs and to the south of the Street of Abundance. Debris from previous excavations was removed, revealing a new necropolis near the Nucerian Gate. Some other important work included the clearing of the House of Julia Felix, originally excavated in 1755–7; the discovery of the painting in the House of Venus, and the finding of the Garden of the Fugitives, containing one of the most harrowing examples of a Pompeian family in its death-throes. In 1961 Alfonso de Franciscis took over the direction of the excavations, and immediately initiated a new drive for the systematic conservation of buildings already excavated – for weather and weeds are no respecters of frescoes and tessellated pavements. Then in 1967 Maiuri died and De Franciscis succeeded him as Superintendent of Antiquities in Southern Italy.

During the last quarter century the excavations at Herculaneum have necessarily produced the more dramatic results. Here, just because so much remains to be uncovered, there is still an enigma. On the other hand, because of the state of preservation of furniture, you also tend to get a more exact idea of a domestic interior than you do at Pompeii. De Franciscis initiated a campaign to secure houses in Resina overlooking the site and have their inhabitants moved to new accommodation. As a result between 1966 and 1967 he was able to start work on the Decumanus Maximus, or main street, running east to west from the Palaestra to the Basilica.

The street is forty feet wide, and on each side there are pavements of ten to twelve feet. It is tantalizing to be faced at one end by a blank wall of solidified mud, very probably concealing the Forum. This area was the commercial centre, containing some of the oldest houses. One of the most important of recent discoveries here is the House of Tuscan Colonnades, which – like the Houses of the Bicentenary and the Wooden Partition – belonged to members of the class of less affluent patricians. Near an archway is the very interesting College of the Augustales, officials responsible for the imperial cult; this building also contained one of Herculaneum's few skeletons.

In 1968 systematic work began on the Palaestra. The Bourbons had dug into it in many places, badly damaging the main entrance but revealing most of one colonnaded portico and a small swimming-pool – you can still see some of their tunnels, massive and rather grim. The whole extent was 360 by 260 feet but most has still to be uncovered, and indeed the pathway for visiting tourists runs right above it. In the centre of the Palaestra there was another large swimming-pool, cruciform in shape, with a five-headed bronze serpent in the middle – still *in situ,* though deep in its hollowed cave. A large apsidal hall, where a statue of Hercules probably stood, and where athletes were received, leads off the colonnade nearest to the town.

82. *Flour mills at Pompeii; the holes were for shafts which were probably turned by donkeys.*

83. *Restoration work in the* atrium *at Oplantis.*

The restoration of the Suburban Baths, unique in layout and decoration, began in 1971. Most of the grandest houses were in this area. The Samnite House, in the centre of the main part of the present excavations, was obviously once very impressive, containing a peristyle, and it is still possible to see how greatly it was altered in Roman times. Another very old house is that of the Bronze Herm, with an *atrium* in the Etruscan style. This one was middle class. Space was obviously the problem with most middle-class houses in Herculaneum. Gardens had to be dispensed with and were turned into courtyards, sometimes with grottoes. Occasionally staircases ran from these courtyards to upper floors. Other examples of middle-class houses are to be seen at the Houses of the Skeleton, the Two Atriums, Neptune and Amphitrite, the Beautiful Courtyard and the Carbonized Furniture. In most cases, of course, the rooms in these houses are small, and – to give the illusion of space – richly decorated.

Herculaneum also contains two examples of plebeian dwellings. One is an apartment house with a frontage of 260 feet. Its present height is 40 feet but it was

84. *The Rape of Europa; fresco found at Pompeii, now in the Naples Museum.*

probably very much higher – in Rome such buildings were five or six storeys. The other is the Trellis House, an extraordinarily flimsy structure where furniture has nevertheless been miraculously preserved.

There is no question which shop in Herculaneum should be singled out. The one at the entrance to the House of Neptune and Amphitrite is perhaps the best preserved from all antiquity. Beans are on the counter, charcoal is in the stove, a lamp is on the hook, *amphorae* are on the racks. Everything is just as it was when Vesuvius erupted in August 79. The owner must have been a man of great taste – one is reminded of Renaissance merchants – for the courtyard contains one of the most splendid examples of mosaic decorations in either Herculaneum or Pompeii: hunting scenes surrounded by festoons of flowers and fruit, and surmounted by theatrical masks and a head of Silenus.

The Forum, temples and necropolis are yet to be uncovered. There is still so much more to be found at Herculaneum. Will, for instance, the villa of the elder Pliny's friend Rectina some day be disclosed to us?

In the first volumes of the *Antichità* the names of Portici, Resina and Civita naturally recur frequently as the places where originals of the engravings were

found. The other place mentioned is Gragnano, in other words the ancient
Stabiae. Some of the most renowned frescoes now kept at the Naples museum
were found there between 1738 and 1782, and presumably most of them came
from the building variously known as the Villa of Ariadne or San Martino at
Varano – a paradise of a situation, if you can shut your eyes to Castellamare
below. No wonder Cicero was enthusiastic about Stabiae. The story of Libero
d'Orsi's excavations there, beginning in 1950, is an exciting one, and all credit
must be given to his enthusiasm and perseverance, not to mention his charm of
manner and the encouragement from Maiuri. His conviction that Stabiae must
lie in that area was immediately vindicated with astounding results. Very shortly
afterwards two other big villas were discovered near by, the Villa of Poseidon and
the one variously known as the Villa of the Obsidian Vases or the Spiral Columns
(or, alternatively, San Marco). Only the outside of the former is shown to
visitors, but the other is a truly magnificent affair, in proportions worthy to rank
with the Villa of the Papyri.

85. *The* apodyterium *(undressing-room) and the ante-room leading from the*
Palaestra of the Stabian Baths, Pompeii.

86. *A replica of the statue of the god that stood outside the Temple of Apollo,
Pompeii, next to the Forum; Vesuvius in the background.*

Libero d'Orsi has created a little museum at Castellamare. Some of the main prizes – such as the obsidian vases, inlaid with Egyptian designs in gold and lapis – had to be sent to Naples. However, d'Orsi's museum does contain some outstanding (though decidedly melancholy) portraits, with a three-dimensional quality that makes them far superior to similar work found at Pompeii or Herculaneum. Indeed the artist's style has been compared to that of Romney.

The Villa of Ariadne had some fifty rooms and an immense terrace overlooking the Bay to Vesuvius. John Martin's impression of the eruption of 79 might almost have been painted there. One of the attractions of visiting the villa is the way in, through a farmyard and orange groves, past trellised vines, maize, and a friendly guard dog living in a barrel.

The painting of the sleeping Ariadne in the great *triclinium* has, with some justification, been likened to a Renaissance deposition. In other rooms there are frescoes of sea-monsters and birds, some like modern wallpaper designs, occasionally – alas – damaged by Bourbon pick-axes. As for the Villa of the Vases, the scale is so large that one wonders whether it could have been built, or enlarged, as a health resort. You enter a huge *atrium,* where again there are sea-monsters, birds and garlands in addition to a well-preserved *lararium.* Then comes a *frigidarium,* decorated with gymnasts, battling cupids and a boxer in repose. Next to it there is a *caldarium.* You emerge into an enormous peristyle with thirty white columns, in the centre of which there is a swimming-pool, thirty feet long. And this is by no means the end, for beyond there are bas-reliefs and a galaxy of paintings: trees, a winged Fortune, a Perseus, Europa, an hermaphrodite. Then, lo, on a higher level there is another wing, with the famous spiral columns, their fluting going in alternate directions to give the illusion of movement, and more paintings . . .

The venerable Libero d'Orsi is rightly proud of his excavations, and lucky visitors may meet him in his museum.

Between 1839 and 1840 there was some digging, evidently without much success, at Torre Annunziata. More soundings were made in the same area in 1964. It was soon realized that the lost site of Oplontis had been discovered. The result has been one of the archaeological sensations of recent years.

The problem at Oplontis is even more complicated than at Herculaneum, for the excavations are hemmed in by apartment blocks and other houses, and a road runs over an important section. At present only one large villa has been found, and indeed Oplontis may just have consisted of this one building. It seems very probable that the house belonged to Poppaea, Nero's wife, whose family also owned property at Pompeii, including the Houses of Menander and the Golden Cupids.

Fifty-three rooms have so far been cleared. The villa seems to have been far

87. *Mosaic of parakeets and a dove at a drinking-bath; Naples Museum.*

more of a town house in conception than a country villa on the Stabian lines. To many visitors it will give one of the most vivid ideas of what a wealthy Roman provincial house was like, from the architectural point of view. A particular point of interest is the very fact of its resemblance to buildings that appear in frescoes, hitherto considered as mere artistic fancies. Originally it had been built in the first century BC, but later it was altered and entirely surrounded by a portico, with two huge pillars at the main garden entrance. There certainly was an upper storey, but it is impossible to say now what extent of the house is covered.

Apart from its great size, which can only be guessed at, since at least half the western side disappears under the road, the extraordinary thing about Oplontis is the decoration of the walls, mostly of the second style and with a unity in its designs comparable to the Villa of the Mysteries and that of Sinistor at Boscoreale. The paintings are nearly all architectural; weird, elaborate, richly coloured, full of peculiar conceits mixed with beautiful *trompe l'œil* details like bowls of fruit and birds. The very name Oplontis sounds exotic, and these paintings are entirely appropriate to it.

As usual many of the rooms are very small, but there are some huge ones, like the saloon into which you enter from the garden. Behind the saloon is another enclosed garden, its walls painted with vegetation. Then there is the *atrium,* with dark red walls on which are painted yellow fluted or marbled columns, doors with figures on them like angels and studded with blue, and fantastic shields which help to give an illusion of depth. But the paintings here are not so amazing as the *triclinium* with its mock courtyard gate, surmounted by winged sea-horses and flanked by great garlanded pillars on which crouch two winged centaurs.

88. *The Empress Poppaea's villa at Oplontis. Originally built in about 50 BC and now one of the archaeological sensations of recent years.*

Professor De Franciscis thinks both rooms could well have been painted by the Boscoreale artist.

It is a temptation to try to describe other paintings – pink and green colonnades receding into blue sky, behind peacocks perched on balustrades and theatrical masks; third style designs of a nereid riding a sea-bull, a flying swan, a silver urn, on crimson ceilings picked out with geometrical designs, and so on. Most of the most important rooms were on the eastern side, which also included the kitchen, supplying heat for the baths. On the west there were quarters for the slaves, chiefly Greek, judging from graffiti (such as 'Beryllos remember' and 'Be ashamed of yourself'). Apparently the house was being redecorated at the time of the eruption – either the furniture had not yet been moved in, or it had been salvaged in good time. No human skeletons were found there, and no animal's except a cat's. It has been estimated that 1·80 metres of *lapilli* and dust fell on the site and that this in turn was covered by five metres of mud. So Oplontis suffered the double fate of Pompeii and Herculaneum.

89. *In the* tepidarium *of the Forum Baths, Pompeii.*

90. *In the Small Theatre, Pompeii.*

The speculation now is whether figured subjects will be discovered again, as at the Mysteries and Boscoreale. We impatiently await developments.

Some final words about Vesuvius. Internal noises and rumblings are still heard, and the Observatory registers up to ten *microterremoti*, or mini-earthquakes, a month. Pozzuoli is still rising; it rose a metre in 1970. Work is being done on the possible relation of atmosphere to eruptions. There is a theory that eruptions could be caused by carbon dioxide generated by limestone. Other volcanoes in

the Mediterranean have shown that their magmas absorbed large quantities of limestone before eruption. Magmas can also contain water in solution in significant amounts – indeed the importance of water in eruptions was recognized in the early nineteenth century by Scrope and Lyell. Another last century theory, about water seepage, possibly from the sea, has lost credibility, however, and there is evidence now that 'juvenile' water is an original constituent of magma.

Volcanic gases and pyroclastic deposits continue to be studied. Dr George Walker surmises that the grey pumice grains in the 79 eruption would have contained less gas than the white, and as it also indicates increased vigour so it would have had the greatest depth of origin, for the grey contains a larger proportion of limestone fragments. As has been mentioned earlier in this book, it is considered that the depth of Vesuvius's magma chamber is five, or even six kilometres below sea-level. The fragments in the white pumice grains, however, indicate that they come from about one kilometre below. It is also thought that the chamber is cylindrical in shape and relatively narrow, possible only 350 metres in diameter.

It is clear that an eruption is unlikely without a warning earthquake. This earthquake could of course be severe, or there could be a series of small tremors mounting in intensity. In any case we can rely on the Observatory to give us warning. At least this silence is a reminder that volcanoes can change their habits. Meanwhile, there is no longer any need to struggle up to the crater by mule or on foot, like Mark Twain or Maximilian of Mexico. On fine days there is a jolly chair-lift to carry us over the black moon-landscape, and Espresso coffee (instead of *vino* at the hermitage) to warm us up on our return.

91. *A charming third style wall-painting of an idealized country scene; Naples museum.*

VI

THE STONES OF POMPEII

Pleasure is a personal matter, difficult to define. I am a compulsive ruin-quester, especially round the Mediterranean. I also love Piranesi, and mock ruins, follies and grottoes. I live in a house built on the site of a Cluniac cell, and am forever digging up unusual stones in the hope that they may have been carved by monks.

Henry James suffered from this *Ruinenlust* too. 'A heartless pleasure,' he said, 'and the pleasure, I confess, shows a note of perversity.' Rose Macaulay even thought of using his phrase, 'a heartless pleasure', as a title for her *Pleasure of Ruins*. A morbid pastime perhaps, in a world bent on fracturing itself. Today, as I write, there is news of a new ruin created in Belfast – but not one to draw the sightseers.

Actually, ruin-questing is an escapist pastime, whether one's motives are romantic, archaeological or literary. True, only a few great ruins have become such through being allowed gently to decay, and most have suffered from some sort of violence or other disaster, such as a war or a Dissolution of the Monasteries or dry rot or abandonment through an owner's bankruptcy. The cities – as they are so often called – beneath Vesuvius are unique in interest for many reasons of their own, as I have attempted to indicate in this book. There is nothing else like them. It was also an extraordinary chance that the first major discoveries should have occurred just as artistic taste and fashion were changing.

There is something in human nature that causes people to be fascinated by great disasters, in the sudden wiping out of some large group, composed of sets of individuals – families, lovers, businessmen – all living out their own secret or public destinies. No doubt I have been drawn to Pompeii by this instinct too. Certainly there we have such a situation *par excellence*. The more Pompeii is systematically excavated, the more we can appreciate the personal dramas on that dreadful August day. It is different at Herculaneum. For one thing it has (nowadays) a more beautiful setting. Then there is that curious sense of intrusion. The inhabitants had been able to escape, but had no time to save their belongings. Herculaneum is like a Roman *Mary Celeste*.

It was hardly romantic, some while ago, to be told that Pompeii was 'on strike'. But this was a symptom of a problem occurring all over a country which has such a heavy cultural burden to maintain. After all, Pompeii is but one of many sites in Italy that needs to be protected and conserved. Then there is the question of

further excavations, which are expensive. Perhaps someone with the vision of
Charles Waldstein is once more needed.

The last time I saw Pompeii was on a late autumn afternoon. The crowds were
dwindling. I walked across the threshold of the House of the Faun, and saw the
word *Have* – Welcome – on which so many travellers have remarked. A large
palm tree, with bright orange dates below the leaves, and two cypresses were
growing in the further peristyle, modern touches that made the replica of the
Dancing Faun himself look even smaller and lonelier. I remembered that this had
been an important house as far back as 200 BC and had been altered at least five
times. I saw the paintings of the first – incrustation – style. Goethe's son had
given a party here, in honour of his father's birthday in 1831. I thought of poor
gouty Gell being carried round in his chair, and of old Sir Walter Scott looking at
the Alexander mosaic, and of the scene of a couple kissing in Jensen's *Gradiva*.
Quantities of pots and jewellery had been found here. The courtyard had been full
of *amphorae,* in preparation for the coming vintage no doubt. There had also

92. *A traditional view of Vesuvius, taken early in this century. Monte Summa can
clearly be seen.*

been a few skeletons. Now all the rooms were empty and swept clean. I was the only live person in a once crowded place.

The light was fading. Vesuvius was turning apricot this time. 'The mountain is the genius of the scene,' so Dickens had said, 'the doom and destiny of this beautiful country, biding its time.' Would its turn come again? Would all that I was seeing now be submerged once more? I thought of that other evening, on my first visit to Pompeii in 1944, and of the friends who had been with me, and of the way Fate had been so swift to deal with many of them, and so soon afterwards. The dusk was filling each corner and crevice of the building, just as the *lapilli* and dust had done in 79. I went out, and heard the autumn leaves like Shelley's footfalls pattering through the streets.

94. *Mosaic of tragic mask and fruit; part of a border from the House of the Faun.*

93. *A magnificent wall-mosaic, worked in cubes of glass paste and marble edged with sea-shells, in the House of the Large Fountain, Pompeii.*

NOTES ON THE ILLUSTRATIONS

The decorative border on the title page, drawn by John Goldicutt and engraved by Edward Finden, is taken from *Specimens of Ancient Decorations from Pompeii* by John Goldicutt. Rodwell and Martin, London, 1825. *Ben Weinreb Architectural Books.*

1. The eruption of Vesuvius, 8 August 1779. Terrified people fleeing across the Maddalena bridge. Engraving by Francesco Piranesi, coloured by Jean-Louis Desprez. Francesco Piranesi was the son of the great Giovanni Battista Piranesi who died in 1778. *Trustees of the British Museum.*

2. Visitors to the Temple of Isis, 1778–9. F. Piranesi and J-L. Desprez. *Trustees of the British Museum.*

3. The last eruption of Vesuvius; after the great blow-off, 23 March 1944. Taken by Sgt Dawson from across the Bay of Naples. *Imperial War Museum.*

4. The Forum at Pompeii today; part of the surrounding colonnade. *Photo: Eric de Maré.*

5. The Forum at Pompeii, *c.* 1850. Before 1944 a tail of smoke was nearly always visible from Vesuvius. Drawn by J. J. Wolfensberger, engraved by E. Radcliffe. *Trattoria Terrazza, London.*

6. The Small Theatre at Pompeii. Originally roofed over and intended for intimate concerts or recitations. *Photo: Eric de Maré.*

7. The strangely moving wheel-marks of carts and chariots at Pompeii, with stepping-stones for pedestrians. *Photo: Eric de Maré.*

8. The sumptuous house of the rich brothers Vettii (perhaps freedmen) was excavated 1894–5. Luigi Bazzani's water-colour shows the north-east corner of the peristyle. *Victoria and Albert Museum.*

9. Stepping stones in a main street, Pompeii. The streets were paved with lava blocks. *Photo: Eric de Maré.*

10. The House of Cornelius Rufus during the Mussolini period. The herm of the owner is seen on the left. The beautifully carved supports of a marble table are in the centre. *Paul Popper Ltd.*

11. Giuseppe Fiorelli, director of excavations from 1860 to 1875, invented the system of preserving the shapes of corpses with plaster of Paris. This hand-tinted photograph belonged to Fiorelli. *The Folio Society.*

12. Night view of Vesuvius's eruption, March 1944. Forked lightning was usual during paroxysmal eruptions. *Imperial War Museum.*

13. Italian soldiers and workmen clearing the main street at San Giuseppe below Vesuvius, after the March 1944 eruption. Volcanic ash and *lapilli* are harmful to many crops, but good for vines. Lacrima Cristi is the famous wine produced on the slopes of Vesuvius. *Imperial War Museum.*

14. Two Allied soldiers survey the damage to a school building at San Sebastiano, 1944. *Imperial War Museum.*

15. The Jumping Pig (bronze). The treasures from the Villa of the Papyri are displayed at the Naples Museum. *Photo: Eric de Maré.*

16. Fresco of a maritime villa found at Stabiae. Naples Museum. Portico villas were more suited to the sea-edge. This one appears to have been built on piles or rocks over the sea. *Photo: Eric de Maré.*

17. Luigi Bazzani's impression of fourth style frescoes decorating a room in the then newly discovered House of the Vettii. The central panel shows Bacchus and Ariadne watching a battle between Pan and Cupid. Decorations similar to these obviously inspired the Adam brothers. *Victoria and Albert Museum.*

18. Engraving of the Temple of Isis from a drawing by J-L. Desprez. The 'mystery' religion of Isis was well entrenched at Pompeii, where there were many signs of Egyptian influences. The original temple was almost destroyed in AD 62–3. Paintings and objects found there in the eighteenth century are now in the Naples Museum. *Trustees of the British Museum.*

19. John Martin's view (*c.* 1820) is almost that from the Villa of Ariadne at Stabiae. A larger version of this picture, damaged by flood and dated 1821, is kept at the Tate Gallery. *Coll. Tabley House: Executors of late Lt. Col. J. L. B. Leicester-Warner.*

20. The opera *L'ultimo giorno di Pompei*, music by Giovanni Pacini and libretto by A. L. Tottola, was first given at the San Carlo, Naples, and then at the Scala, Milan, in 1827. Alessandro Sanquirico did the designs for the Scala production. *Coll. Edward Croft-Murray.*

21. The hermit did a good trade in providing refreshments for visitors ascending to the crater.

The island of Capri can be seen on the right. Lithograph by Charles J. Hullmandel from *Twenty-Four Views of Italy* (1818). *Victoria and Albert Museum.*

22. One of the five life-size bronze dancers, *c.* 450 BC, found at the Villa of the Papyri and now in the Naples Museum. The eyes are made of glass paste and the *peplos* shows traces of colour. *Photo: Eric de Maré.*

23. The subterranean theatre at Herculaneum can still be visited by special permission. This illustration is from Miceto de Zamarcois' *La Destruccion de Pompeya*, a sentimental novel based on Bulwer Lytton's book and published in Mexico in 1871. *The Folio Society.*

24. Telephus suckled by a deer. This detail is from one of the three famous frescoes found in the 1730s at the Herculaneum Basilica. Based on a Pergamene painting. Now in Naples Museum. *Photo: Eric de Maré.*

25. Galley-slaves excavating near Herculaneum. The picture shows the depth of the mudflow in AD 79. The royal villa is in the background. From Morghen and Cardon's *84 Vedute di Napoli* (1777). *Victoria and Albert Museum.*

26. *The Cupid Seller* appeared in the *Antichità* vol. III and became a popular motif in Neo-classic designs. This version by J. H. W. Tischbein is in the Goethe Museum at Düsseldorf.

27. The Hermes in Repose is perhaps the best known masterpiece from the Villa of the Papyri. There are four views of it in the *Antichità*, more than of any other object. *Trustees of Sir John Soane's Museum.*

28. James 'Athenian' Stuart's designs anticipated decorations. He visited Pompeii in 1754 and his furniture shows marked Pompeian motifs. It is thought that he may have been influenced by Caylus (1752) and Cochin (1754). *Trustees of the British Museum.*

29. Discovery of a skeleton. An illustration by J. H. Fragonard from the Abbé de Saint-Non's *Voyage pittoresque* (1782). *Trustees of the British Museum.*

30. This exquisite little tripod is only 90 cm high and is now on public view at the Naples Museum. For Neo-classic designers the tripod was the 'greatest revelation' of all (Praz). *Photo: Eric de Maré.*

31. Adam's design for an Etruscan room is like a refined version of frescoes found recently at Oplontis. In the eighteenth century Pompeian motifs were often (and wrongly) called 'Etruscan'. Adam evolved a so-called Etruscan style, with extensive use of Grecian vases (as seen at Osterley). 20 Portman Square is now the Courtauld Institute. *Trustees of Sir John Soane's Museum.*

32. Several of the Pompeian phallic symbols, now in the Gabinetto Segreto, are hung with bells. These *tintinnabula* are thought to have been talismans against the evil eye. (See *The Satyricon* ch. IV for some wild contemporary antics connected with the cult of Priapus.) Engraving from *Antichità* vol. VII. *Trustees of Sir John Soane's Museum.*

33. Angelica Kauffman's portrait etching of Winckelmann: a painted portrait by the same artist is now in the Kunsthaus, Zurich. *Trustees of the British Museum.*

34. Inside the crater of Vesuvius – 'the most horrible chaos that can be imagined' (Shelley). From Morghen and Cardon, *op. cit. Victoria and Albert Museum.*

35. The tomb of the priestess Mamia in the Street of the Tombs, Pompeii. F. Piranesi and J-L. Desprez. *Trustees of the British Museum.*

36. Hamilton's *Campi Phlegraei*, subtitled *Observations on the Volcanoes of the Two Sicilies*, was published in two volumes in 1776, with a supplement in 1779. The artist was Pietro Fabris. Hamilton complained that the frescoes from the Temple were removed at random and 'confounded' with others at Portici. *London Library.*

37. Visitors to the crater described how you could hear, deep down, a sinister noise as of liquids bubbling. From *Encyclopédie ou Dictionnaire Raisonné des Sciences, des Arts et des Métiers* by Denis Diderot and Jean Le Rond d'Alembert. The work was suspended in 1756 for an anti-religious bias. *John Pearman.*

38. These two centaurs, copied from the originals found in the so-called Villa of Cicero, are – like the Villa's bacchantes – among the best known of any Pompeian motifs. They reappear in quantities of medallions, inlaid furniture, porcelain designs, plasterwork and panels during the Neo-classic and Empire period. *Trustees of the British Museum.*

39. *a.* Lava from the 1761 eruption. *b.* Hamilton shows the lava flow to Ferdinand IV and Maria Carolina. From *Campi Phlegraei. London Library.*

40. Sir William Hamilton in the robes of a Knight of the Bath. Oil by David Allan. *National Portrait Gallery.*

41. Engraving by G. Hackert, after the painting by Jacob Philipp Hackert, of the Large Theatre at Pompeii, 1793. The Large Theatre could seat at least 5,000 spectators. *Victoria and Albert Museum.*

42. *The Cupid Seller* by Vien, 1763, now at Fontainebleau. Joseph-Marie Vien and Anton Raphael Mengs were among the first Neo-classic artists to find inspiration in the *Antichità.* Mengs' fake fresco, *Jupiter and Ganymede,* fooled even Winckelmann. *Lauros-Giraudon.*

43. Entrance to Pompeii, *c.* 1778. F. Piranesi and J-L. Desprez. *Trustees of the British Museum.*

44. Robert Adam's design, published in the *Adelphi* magazine 25 January 1776,was never in fact executed. Gryphons recur often on Adam furniture, e.g. the commode in the drawing-room at Osterley (1773), along with sphinxes, scrolls, garlands, urns etc., which appeared generally within geometrical designs – a contrast to the fantastic swirls of the Rococo age. Charles Cameron's work at St Petersburg owed much to Adam, but contained a more direct use of Pompeian, as against Raphaelesque, motifs. The availability of materials such as agate and malachite enabled Cameron to raise Neo-classicism to a magnificent level. *Trustees of Sir John Soane's Museum.*

45. Excavations, 1793. Jacob Philipp Hackert, a German, became court painter in Naples and accompanied Goethe round the Two Sicilies. *Goethe Museum, Düsseldorf.*

46. The treasures of the Portici Museum were removed to Naples because of danger from eruptions. The ithyphallic tripod and one of the equestrian Balbi can be seen in this procession. The Naples Museum was originally built as a cavalry barracks in 1586. F. Piranesi and J-L. Desprez. *Trustees of the British Museum.*

47. The court of the Gladiators' Barracks, originally an annexe to the Large Theatre where spectators could shelter. Over sixty gladiators' skeletons have been found here. *Baynton Williams Prints.*

48. Lady Hamilton, by this time pregnant by Nelson. The floating bacchantes from the 'Villa of Cicero' were among her favourite models for her Attitudes. Drawing by Richard Cosway. *National Portrait Gallery.*

49. The crater, 1832. After the paroxysmal eruption of 1822 the crater was reckoned to be 938 ft deep, but by 1831 the cone was visible from below. Charles Lyell's second volume of *Principles of Geology*, containing the first proper synthesis of Vesuvius's history, was published in 1832. *John Pearman.*

50. Joseph Wright of Derby travelled in Italy between 1773 and 1775. He was deeply impressed by an eruption of Vesuvius and painted this picture on his return. *Derby Museum and Art Gallery.*

51. The lava of 1794, witnessed and reported on by Hamilton, also devastated Resina. This scene shows the flow on the eighth day after the eruption. Engraving by J. Barnett after a drawing by Lady H. Fitzgerald. *Victoria and Albert Museum.*

52. A plate from the 282-piece 'Etruscan Service' (including bacchantes and centaurs) was sent by Ferdinand IV to George III. A new royal porcelain factory was opened at Capo-dimonte in 1770; from 1780 to 1806 it was under the direction of Domenico Venuti. The *Antichità* volumes provided much inspiration for the Wedgwood, Sèvres, Retiro, Doccia and Vienna factories. *By gracious permission of Her Majesty the Queen.*

53. Caroline Murat, Napoleon's youngest sister, was Queen of Naples from 1808 to 1815. She was obsessed by Pompeii and had an almost childish delight in new discoveries, the best of which were carried off to her rooms at Portici. She gave large sums of money towards the excavations. Her taste influenced the distinctive style in Neapolitan Empire furniture (some to be seen at Attingham Park, Shrewsbury). Painting by François Gérard. Château de Malmaison. *Lauros-Giraudon.*

54. Prince Napoleon ('Plon-Plon') began his elaborate 'palais pompéien' or 'Villa Diomède' in 1857. Designed by Alfred-Nicolas Normand, it became – according to Arsène Houssaye's *Confessions* – the 'rendezvous of all Paris, both of the Court and the Arts'. *Le Joueur de flûte*, by Emile Augier, was preceded by Gautier's prologue, *La Femme de Diomède*. Painting by Gustave Boulanger. *Palais de Versailles. Photo: Giraudon.*

55. Sir William Gell by T. Uwins (1830). Gell was Hamilton's successor as the authority on Pompeii. In 1832 he conducted the ailing Sir Walter Scott round the ruins, but found him

'insensible' to antiquarian matters. Scott saw the whole 'with the eye of the poet', repeating 'The City of the Dead! The City of the Dead!' *National Portrait Gallery.*

56. The Street of the Tombs, 1837. Samuel Palmer's unique feeling for landscape had by this time become less (in his words) 'primitive and infantine'. *Victoria and Albert Museum.*

57. Mme de Staël was in Naples between 1804 and 1805. Her *Corinne* (1807), the 'worst great novel ever written', was outstanding both for its place in Romanticism and as a new type of travel literature. Her long descriptions of Pompeii were designed to show that the ruins were important not merely as proving facts but as a stimulus to the imagination. 'Here, for a long time, man lived, loved, suffered and then perished – but where will you find his feelings, his thoughts?' *Musée d'Art et d'Histoire, Geneva.*

58. Edward Bulwer Lytton by H. Pickersgill. *The Last Days of Pompeii* was written under great strain, for Lytton's wife had meanwhile fallen in love with a Neapolitan prince and had had to be brought back to London. Lytton was Secretary for the Colonies between 1858–9 and ennobled in 1866. *National Portrait Gallery.*

59. The original edition of *Pompeiana*, illustrated by John P. Gandy, was published in 1817–19. It was the first comprehensive guide in English. After Lytton's success, Gell wisely brought out a revised, enlarged edition in 1835. *Trustees of Sir John Soane's Museum.*

60. Many of the engravings in *Pompeiana* were based on *camera lucida* drawings. *Trustees of Sir John Soane's Museum.*

61. Vesuvius, 1817. Turner had not yet visited Italy. This painting may have been based on sketches by J. Hakewill. *Mr and Mrs Paul Mellon.*

62. Reconstruction of the House of Actaeon (or Sallust) from *Pompeiana*. Such pictures were fashionable as a result of Thomas Hope's books and designs. The house had been mainly uncovered when Joseph Bonaparte was King of Naples – the start of a period of new enthusiasm, energy and method in the excavations. The fresco of Actaeon was destroyed by bombing in the last war. *Trustees of Sir John Soane's Museum.*

63. Bakery at Pompeii, *c.* 1870, showing mills. In antiquity the miller and the baker were the same person. *The Folio Society.*

64. Queen Victoria visited Pompeii in 1838, when a 'prepared' dig was arranged for her, but the Buckingham Palace Garden-Pavilion, built in 1844 by L. Grüner, was the Prince Consort's idea. The vogue for Pompeian decoration had grown fast in his native Germany, to a more developed degree than in Britain or even France – starting with Ermandshoff's Villa Hamilton (1789) at Worlitz Park, and continuing with the Marmorpalais at Potsdam, Ludwig I's replica house at Aschaffenburg and Klenze's designs for the Maxpalais and Hofgarten arcades (1840) in Munich. The two other rooms in the Buckingham Palace pavilion were decorated with scenes from *Comus* and Walter Scott's novels. The pavilion fell into disrepair and was demolished by Queen Mary in 1928. *Ben Weinreb Architectural Books.*

65. *In the Temple* by Laurence Alma-Tadema. The most famous adaptation, indeed copy, of the sphinx tripod is the ormulu and lapis-lazuli font, designed for the Empress Marie-Louise and now at the Schatzkammer, Vienna. *Sotheby's.*

66. Climbing Vesuvius; muleback was better. The return journey was 'a labour of only four minutes', involving such prodigious strides as would 'almost have shamed the performance of him of the seven-league boots' (Mark Twain). *John Pearman.*

67. The House of the Hunt (where some pre-Roman traces are still visible) by Luigi Bazzani. *Victoria and Albert Museum.*

68. Silver cup from the Villa La Pisanella, Boscoreale. One of a pair, showing skeletons and with an exhortation to enjoy life while you still have it. *Musée du Louvre: cliché Musées Nationaux, Paris.*

69. Excavating the House of the Vettii in 1894 – with more system and energy than had been customary in Bourbon times. *H. Roger Viollet, Paris.*

70. Skeletons of the family of Obellius Firmus. *H. Roger Viollet, Paris.*

71. The serpent here is shown in the act of eating the funeral offerings. Every large dwelling usually had a *lararium* or shrine to the household gods. *Photo: Eric de Maré.*

72. The Villa of Diomede was, after the Villa of the Mysteries, the most important and luxurious suburban building at Pompeii. Excavated (or, rather, desecrated) between 1771 and 1774, it created considerable archaeological and

literary excitement. Some of its paintings reached the Portici Museum. Drawn by John Goldicutt and engraved by Edward Finden. *Ben Weinreb Architectural Books.*

73. The *Thermopolium* in the Street of the Abundance, Pompeii. Asellina and her friends entertained customers in the room above. *H. Roger Viollet, Paris.*

74. Cast of a corpse of a suffocated Pompeian, now a museum exhibit. *Photo: Eric de Maré.*

75. The House of the Stags was one of the richest and most modern houses in Herculaneum – airy and cool, with a beautiful view of the Bay. *Photo: Eric de Maré.*

76. The so-called 'Arch of Nero', sometimes known as the 'Arch of Caligula' or 'Germanicus', Pompeii. *Victoria and Albert Museum.*

77. The connecting arch between the Large and Small Theatres, Pompeii. *Photo: Eric de Maré.*

78. The bronze deer from the Villa of the Papyri: sent to Berlin in 1943 as a birthday present for Goering. *Photo: Eric de Maré.*

79. The Forum of Herculaneum still lies hidden beneath Resina, as presumably do temples, the amphitheatre, the necropolis and brothels. *Photo: Eric de Maré.*

80. Pallas Athene. This archaic marble statue is in impressive contrast to the other mostly naturalistic pieces – about ninety in all – found at the Villa of the Papyri. *Photo: Eric de Maré.*

81. The serpent's five heads sprayed water into a cruciform pool. *Photo: Eric de Maré.*

82. Flour mills at Pompeii. The lower stone was a fixture, the top one rotated by shafts. Both were made from volcanic lava. *Photo: Eric de Maré.*

83. Oplontis. The background shows second style frescoes of columns and doors painted on rich shades of red. *Photo: Sunday Times.*

84. *The Rape of Europa. Photo: Eric de Maré.*

85. The Stabian Baths were the oldest at Pompeii and contain beautiful stucco work. Water-colour by Luigi Bazzani. *Victoria and Albert Museum.*

86. The Temple of Apollo, surrounded by a portico of forty-eight columns, stood on an ancient site and was probably the chief sanctuary at Pompeii. The statue shows Apollo as an archer. *Photo: Eric de Maré.*

87. Doves drinking: one of the most charming mosaics at the Naples Museum. *Photo: Eric de Maré.*

88. The villa at Oplontis was built in the Roman tradition with some Hellenistic elements. Systematic excavations only began in 1964, but the site of the building first noticed in 1834 when an Englishman, Colonel Robinson, was employed in some excavations for a thermal establishment. *Photo: Eric de Maré.*

89. The well preserved *tepidarium* in the men's section of the Forum Baths, Pompeii. The ceiling is supported by telamons. *Photo:Eric de Maré.*

90. There is an extraordinary atmosphere of peace and relaxation in the Small Theatre, or Odeon, at Pompeii. Two telamons in tufa support each end of the auditorium's parapets. *Photo: Eric de Maré.*

91. These Arcadian scenes were popular in the period before the earthquake of AD 62. *Photo: Eric de Maré.*

92. This view is taken from the Immacolatella landing-stage in Naples. *Photo: Alinari.*

93. These elaborate fountains were popular in the Post-Augustan period. The cupid with a dolphin is a copy of the bronze original. *Photo: Eric de Maré.*

94. The House of the Faun is famous for the mosaics found there, and in particular for a scene of Nile fauna and the great Battle between Alexander and Darius at Issus (now in the Naples Museum), a second century BC masterpiece. *Photo: Eric de Maré.*

A . Rottura fatta dalla Lava all'Atrio del Cavallo.
B . Vallone de Morti.
C . Lava Vecchia.
D . Territorio de Matroni Magliola, e Vitelli.
E . Bosco d'Ottaiano.

F . Valle del Fruscio.
G . Casino di Bonincontri.
H . Osteria d:a la Quercia.
I . Osteria del Baron Maßa, detta le Caselle.

Veduta del Corso della Lava eruttata Dal

K . Casino del Baron Maßa, suoi Territori.
L . Casa di Carlo Avezzato ove terminò la Lava.
M . Strada di Poggio Marino

Ignazio Vernet inventò, e delineò.

Agl'Ill.mi ed Ecc.mi Sig.r Cavalier Tomaso Vorsley Baronetto della Gran Brett